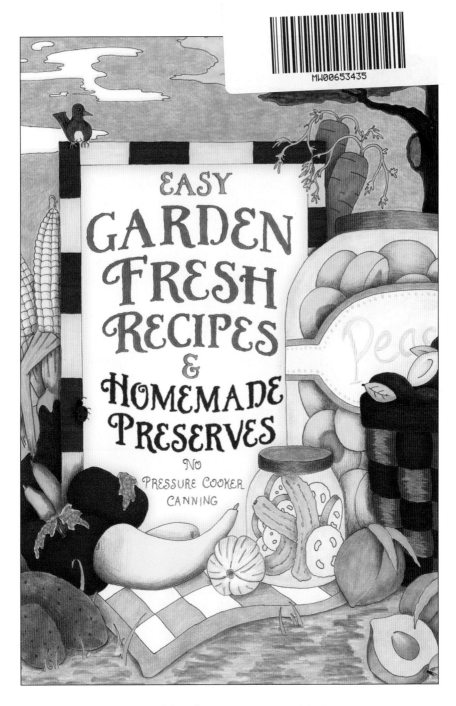

EASY
GARDEN
FRESH
RECIPES
&
HOMEMADE
PRESERVES

NO
PRESSURE COOKER
CANNING

Cookbook Resources, LLC
Highland Village, Texas

Easy Garden Fresh Recipes & Homemade Preserves
No Pressure Cooker Canning

Printed November 2012

© Copyright 2012 by Cookbook Resources, LLC

International Standard Book Number: 978-1-59769-201-4

Library of Congress Control Number:

Library of Congress Cataloging-in-Publication Data

Easy Homemade Preserves by Helen Hughes Hawkins

Cover and design by Rasor Design

Edited, Designed and Published in the United States of America
and Manufactured in China by
Cookbook Resources, LLC
541 Doubletree Drive
Highland Village, Texas 75077

Toll free 866-229-2665

www.cookbookresources.com

Bringing Family and Friends to the Table

Garden Fresh and Homemade!

The best fruits and vegetables come from your own backyard, or better yet, the backyard garden of a relative or best friend. Whether you grow your own fruits and vegetables or make regular visits to the local farmers' markets and specialty stores, you recognize the delicious tastes and healthy benefits of fresh foods.

Easy Garden Fresh Recipes & Homemade Preserves is an entertaining cookbook with easy ways to enjoy fresh fruits and vegetables. It's a great introduction to cooking fresh and simple canning. Time commitments and skill levels are minimal, but the rewards are super.

It just makes sense to know where your food comes from and to know what goes into the food you eat. It also makes sense to get the most out of your food dollars and the most nutrition out of the foods you serve.

But, the best of all is we create many memories for family and friends that last a lifetime. Whether it's learning to drive on a dirt road to the strawberry lady's house and making strawberry jam afterward or making cookies with Grandma or simply eating together at the kitchen table, family memories are the most precious of all.

Easy Garden Fresh Recipes & Homemade Preserves is loaded with easy, delicious recipes that serve up the best homemade memories.

The best memories are made in the kitchen.

Contents

Easy Garden Fresh Recipes

Contents
Homemade Preserves

Appetizers, Beverages, Breakfast & Brunch

Contents

Tropical Mango Salsa

*Serve with grilled pork or swordfish or tuna steaks
or even with bruschetta for a tasty appetizer.*

2 large very ripe mangoes, peeled, cubed
½ cup diced purple onion
¼ cup chopped fresh cilantro
2 - 3 tablespoons freshly squeezed lime juice

Stir together all ingredients. Cover salsa with
plastic wrap.

Refrigerate for 30 minutes to blend flavors. Makes
about 1 cup.

*TIP: Bell peppers, green onions or pineapple are good
    mixed with mango, too.*

**The most interesting information comes
from children, for they tell all they know
and then stop.**
                                              -Mark Twain

Cilantro Pico de Gallo

1 whole jalapeno, seeded, diced*
½ cup minced fresh cilantro
½ red onion, chopped
2 large tomatoes, chopped
Juice of 2 limes
½ teaspoon garlic salt
½ teaspoon seasoned salt

● Stir together all ingredients and ¼ teaspoon pepper or to taste. Cover and refrigerate to blend flavors.

● Serve with tortilla chips, over guacamole salad or over grilled fish or pork. Makes about 1 cup.

*TIP: Wear rubber gloves when removing seeds from jalapenos.

Children who eat at home almost every night during the week are more likely to make better grades and perform better in school than those who do not. In a Readers' Digest *national poll of high school seniors in 1994, Lou Harris reported higher school scores among seniors who ate with their families. He also found that high school seniors were happier with themselves and prospects for the future than seniors who did not eat at home regularly.*

Sunshine Guacamole

4 ripe avocados
3 tablespoons lime juice
2 tablespoons diced fresh tomatoes
1 clove garlic, minced
¼ cup minced cilantro
Hot pepper sauce or minced jalapeno pepper

🍅 Peel and coarsely mash avocados, but leave some bite-sized pieces. Mix all ingredients in bowl except pepper sauce.

🍅 Add a little salt, pepper and a little hot sauce to taste and serve immediately. Makes about 1 pint.

God made rainy days so gardeners could get housework done.

Prosciutto and Melon Bites

This is so simple, but the flavors are so heavenly.

1 large cantaloupe or honeydew melon
1 lime, juiced
¼ - ½ pound thinly sliced prosciutto
Balsamic vinegar

● Remove cantaloupe rind and cut into bite-size pieces. Place into container and pour lime juice over cantaloupe and toss well.

● Wrap piece of prosciutto around each cantaloupe bite. Sprinkle with balsamic vinegar and serve. Serves 6 to 8.

The secret of staying young is to live honestly, eat slowly and lie about your age.
                                                        –Lucille Ball

Peppered Bacon-Zucchini Rolls

2 zucchini
12 slices peppered bacon
2 ounces goat cheese or ¼ cup whipped cream cheese
1 teaspoon lemon juice
1 teaspoon dried parsley

Slice zucchini lengthwise about ¼ inch thick. Fry bacon, but not crisp and still soft; drain well. Mix cheese, lemon juice and parsley.

Arrange bacon on each zucchini slice. Spread cheese down middle of bacon and roll up. Secure with toothpick if needed.

Cook on sprayed grill over medium hot fire just until grill marks show and zucchini is tender. Remove from grill before cheese melts. Makes about 12 rolls.

Two cannibals were eating a clown.
One said to the other, "Does this taste
funny to you?"

Fresh Garlic Mushrooms

1 tablespoon extra virgin olive oil
2 tablespoons butter
¾ cup Italian breadcrumbs
3 cloves garlic, peeled, minced
¼ teaspoon oregano
Cracked black pepper
18 large button mushrooms, stemmed
¼ cup grated parmesan cheese

● Preheat oven to 400°. Heat olive oil and butter in
  skillet over medium heat. Add breadcrumbs, stir to
  coat and cook about 5 minutes.

● Add garlic, oregano, a little salt and fresh ground
  black pepper and saute until garlic is translucent.
  Stuff each mushroom with breadcrumb mixture and
  sprinkle parmesan on top.

● Place in sprayed 9 x 13-inch baking pan. Bake for
  20 minutes or until mushrooms are tender. Serve hot
  or at room temperature. Serves 10 to 12.

*We're always the same age on the
inside.*
                                    –Gertrude Stein

Garden Stuffed Mushrooms

1 (12 ounce) carton large button mushrooms
½ cup seasoned stuffing mix
¼ cup (½ stick) butter, softened
¼ cup minced celery
¼ cup minced zucchini
¼ cup minced red bell pepper
2 tablespoons crumbled goat cheese

Remove stems from mushrooms. Mix stuffing, butter, celery, zucchini, and dash of salt and pepper. Stuff mixture into mushroom cavities.

Cook on sprayed grill away from direct heat with lid closed for about 10 minutes or until mushrooms are tender and grill marks appear.

Sprinkle with goat cheese. Serves about 4 to 6.

The difference between fiction and reality? Fiction has to make sense.

Tomato-Basil Bruschetta

1 (16 ounce) loaf Italian bread
Butter
8 - 12 roma tomatoes, minced, drained
3 - 4 cloves garlic, peeled, minced
3 - 4 tablespoons minced plus several leaves fresh basil
½ (3 ounce) can diced black olives
Virgin olive oil

Preheat oven to 300°.

Slice bread in thick pieces, butter one side and lay, buttered side up on sprayed baking sheet. Bake until slices are crispy.

Drain chopped tomatoes again and place in small bowl. Add garlic, basil, black olives, a little salt and pepper, and just enough olive oil to coat all ingredients. Stir to mix well.

Place several tablespoons tomato mixture on each bread slice just before serving. Garnish with whole basil leaves. Serves 6 to 8.

TIP: *If you like lots of ingredients on bread, double the recipe. Taste the tomato mixture for the right seasonings.*

Island Fruit Smoothie

½ cup low-fat milk or soy milk
1 (6 ounce) carton low-fat vanilla yogurt
1 banana, quartered
1 cup fresh blueberries or blackberries
1 cup sliced fresh strawberries or raspberries

Combine all ingredients in blender. Process until
smooth. Makes 2 smoothies.

TIP: *Use low-fat milk, yogurt, soy milk and tofu instead*
of whole milk for smoothies. There is no difference in
the taste and flavor of smoothies.

Raw foods have more enzymes, nutrients
and vitamins than cooked foods. You tend
to eat less than you eat of cooked foods,
but you feel fuller with raw foods and are
getting more nutrition.

Funky Kingston Town

1 cup low-fat milk or soy milk
1 (6 ounce) carton low-fat vanilla yogurt
2 peaches, peeled, chopped
2 mangoes, peeled, chopped
1 banana, peeled, sliced
8 baby carrots

🍅 Place all ingredients in blender. Add 1 cup crushed ice and blend until almost smooth.

🍅 Serve immediately. Makes 2 smoothies.

TIP: When you mix fruit with vegetables, the flavor of the fruit will overpower the flavor of the vegetables.

Mango trees can grow to be 65 feet tall, live to be 300 years old and still bear fruit. Its taproot can grow to 20 feet below the surface.

When ripe, mangoes are soft and very juicy. The best place to eat a really ripe, really juicy mango is in a bathtub!

Green Gorilla

*Don't let the color throw you. This is delicious and
so full of nutrition. Fruit masks the taste of
vegetables so don't tell the kids about the veggies.*

2 cups fresh spinach, stemmed
1 medium ripe avocado, peeled, pitted
¾ cup frozen mango slices
¾ cup frozen pineapple chunks or kiwifruit halves

● Pour ¾ cup water and 4 ice cubes into blender and
add all ingredients.

● Process until smooth and serve immediately.
Makes 2 smoothies.

*Laughing is good exercise. It's like
jogging on the inside.*

-Anonymous

Gazpacho in a Glass

3 large tomatoes, quartered
1 (16 ounce) can tomato juice, chilled
½ cup vegetable stock, chilled
1 green bell pepper, cored, quartered
1 small onion, peeled, quartered
½ medium cucumber, peeled, sliced
¼ cup red wine vinegar
½ teaspoon garlic powder

🍅 Puree tomatoes in blender. Add remaining
   ingredients except garlic powder and blend for
   about 20 seconds.

🍅 Taste mixture and season with a little garlic powder,
   salt and pepper. Taste again and adjust seasonings,
   if needed. Refrigerate for about 30 minutes. Makes
   3 to 4 servings.

*Nine out of every ten tomatoes grown
in the U.S. are grown in California. In
addition over 85% of all home gardeners in
the U.S. grow tomatoes.*

Winter Spiced Cider

1 gallon fresh apple cider
2 cups fresh orange juice
¼ cup maple syrup
½ teaspoon lemon extract
5 cinnamon sticks
3 teaspoons whole cloves
½ teaspoon whole allspice berries

● Combine apple cider, orange juice, maple syrup and lemon extract in large roasting pan.

● Place cinnamon sticks, cloves and allspice in piece of cheesecloth. Bring up corners, tie with string to form bag and add to roasting pan.

● Cook over medium heat (do not boil) for 15 to 20 minutes. Discard spice bag. Serves 16 to 22.

TIP: Star anise is an attractive garnish.

The top six apple-producing states in the U.S. are Washington, New York, Michigan, California, Pennsylvania and Virginia. Washington is responsible for more than half the U.S. total production.

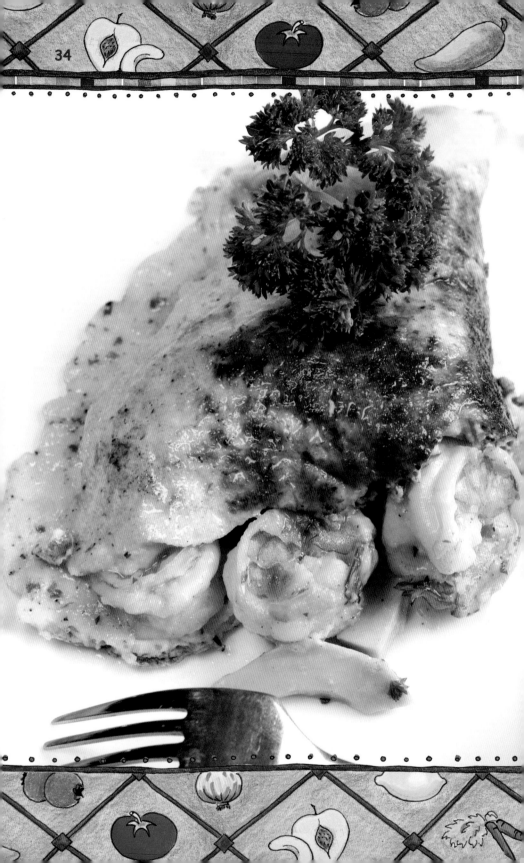

Shrimp and Avocado Stuffed Omelet

6 large eggs
½ cup milk
½ pound small cooked shrimp, veined
1 large avocado, seeded, peeled, diced
¾ cup shredded Monterey Jack cheese
¾ cup seeded, minced, drained tomatoes
¼ cup minced parsley
½ cup sliced mushrooms

● Beat eggs with milk in bowl vigorously. Pour into large, sprayed skillet. Cook over low heat until eggs begin to firm up. Slide eggs around in skillet while cooking.

● Gently mix shrimp, avocado, cheese, tomatoes, parsley and mushrooms in bowl and spread over one-half of eggs. Use spatula to lift other half of eggs onto cheese mixture. Cook until firm on the inside and cheese melts. Serves 4 to 6.

I'm a great believer of luck, and I find the harder I work, the more I have of it.
-Thomas Jefferson

Garden Fresh Summer Omelet

½ cup chopped green beans
½ cup chopped green bell pepper
1 tablespoon oil
½ cup diced tomatoes, drained
2 tablespoons chopped basil
8 eggs
¼ cup milk
⅓ cup shredded parmesan or cheddar cheese

🍅 Cook green beans and bell pepper in oil in skillet for about 3 minutes or just until tender. Stir in tomatoes and basil, cook for 1 to 2 minutes and drain.

🍅 In separate bowl, combine eggs, milk, and a little salt and pepper; whisk to mix. Add vegetable mixture and pour into sprayed skillet. Cook over medium-high heat until center is almost set.

🍅 Flip half on top of other half and sprinkle with cheese. Serve when cheese melts.   Serves 4.

TIP: If your skillet isn't big enough for one large omelet, divide mixture in half and make 2 omelets.

Asparagus Quiche

1 (9 inch) frozen piecrust
¼ cup (½ stick) butter
3 tablespoons flour
1½ cups milk
4 eggs
1 pound fresh asparagus, trimmed, chopped
½ cup shredded Swiss cheese
¼ cup breadcrumbs

Preheat oven to 450°. Place several sheets of heavy-duty foil in piecrust and over edge. Bake for about 5 minutes. Remove from oven, discard foil and bake for additional 5 minutes.

Melt butter in saucepan and stir in flour and a little salt. Stir to dissolve all lumps. Cook over medium heat and gradually pour in milk. Continue to stir until mixture thickens.

Add remaining ingredients except breadcrumbs and beat. Pour into piecrust and sprinkle breadcrumbs over quiche.

Bake for about 30 minutes or until knife inserted in center comes out clean. Cool slightly, slice into wedges and serve warm. Serves 6.

A diet rich in fruits and vegetables helps prevent chronic diseases such as heart disease, type 2 diabetes, stroke and some cancers.

Diets rich in fiber (such as beans) help decrease the risk of coronary artery disease.

Diets rich in potassium (potatoes, tomato paste and puree, white beans) help maintain healthy blood pressure.

Diets rich in Vitamin A (pumpkin, carrots, spinach, greens, winter squash) help prevent infections and maintain healthy eyes and skin.

Diets rich in Vitamin C (strawberries, bell peppers, sweet potatoes, tomatoes, broccoli, oranges) help maintain healthy teeth and gums.

Zucchini Quiche

1 (9 inch) frozen piecrust
¼ cup (½ stick) butter
3 tablespoons flour
1½ cups milk
4 eggs
1 pound zucchini, chopped
½ cup shredded Swiss cheese
¼ cup breadcrumbs

🍅 Preheat oven to 450°. Place heavy-duty foil over edge of piecrust. Bake for about 5 minutes. Remove from oven, discard foil and bake for additional 5 minutes.

🍅 Melt butter in saucepan and stir in flour and a little salt. Stir to dissolve all lumps. Cook over medium heat and gradually pour in milk. Continue to stir until mixture thickens.

🍅 Add remaining ingredients except breadcrumbs and beat. Pour into piecrust and sprinkle breadcrumbs over quiche.

🍅 Bake for about 30 minutes or until knife inserted in center comes out clean. Cool slightly, slice into wedges and serve warm. Serves 6.

Baked Bananas

4 firm bananas
¾ cup (1½ sticks) butter, melted
¾ cup packed brown sugar
1 teaspoon vanilla

🍎 Preheat oven to 350°.

🍎 Halve bananas lengthwise and peel each half
carefully; set aside the peels for presentation. Slice
the bananas and arrange in sprayed baking dish.

🍎 In saucepan, combine butter and brown sugar and
heat just enough to mix well. Stir in vanilla and pour
over bananas.

🍎 Bake for 15 to 20 minutes or until bananas are soft
and sauce is bubbling. Arrange the banana slices in
the peels to serve. Serves 8.

Why are bananas never lonely?
Because they hang around in bunches.

Why did the banana go out with
a prune?
Because he couldn't get a date.

Breakfast Fruit Parfait

*Red huckleberries are always called huckleberries,
but other species may be called blueberries. Choose
the best berries from your local farmers' market.*

1 cup flavored or plain yogurt
1 tablespoon honey
2 cups sliced fresh fruit and mixed berries

Mix yogurt and honey in bowl and top with fruit. Or
make as individual servings in parfait glasses or cups
and layer ingredients. Serves 2.

TIP: Chopped nuts and/or granola are great additions.

**Honey is the only edible food for
humans that never spoils. It is still edible
even after thousands of years.**

Fresh Blueberry Muffins

1¼ cups sugar
2 cups flour
1½ teaspoons baking powder
½ cup (1 stick) butter, softened
1 egg, beaten
1 cup milk
1½ cups fresh blueberries
½ cup chopped pecans, optional

● Preheat oven to 375°.

● Combine sugar, flour, baking powder and ½ teaspoon
   salt in large bowl. Cut in softened butter until
   mixture is coarse.

● Stir in egg and milk and beat well. Gently fold in
   blueberries and pecans, but do not beat.

● Spoon into sprayed, floured muffin cups (or cups with
   paper liners) and bake for 35 minutes or until light
   brown. Makes 12 muffins.

*Berries are one of nature's best
pleasures. They are easy and fun to eat,
loaded with vitamin C, calcium, magnesium,
folate and potassium, and low in calories.*

Fresh Zucchini Bread

3 eggs
2 cups sugar
1 cup oil
2 teaspoons vanilla
2 cups grated zucchini with peel
2 cups flour
1 tablespoon cinnamon
1 teaspoon baking soda
¼ teaspoon baking powder
1 cup chopped nuts

Preheat oven to 325°.

Beat eggs until fluffy and add sugar, oil and vanilla. Beat until thick and lemon-colored.

Stir in zucchini, flour, cinnamon, baking soda, baking powder and 1 teaspoon salt.

Fold in nuts and spoon into 2 sprayed, floured loaf pans. Bake for 55 minutes. Cool in pan for about 10 minutes before removing from loaf pan. Serves 8 to 10.

Hard work doesn't hurt anyone, but I don't want to take any chances.

–Anonymous

Apple-Banana Bread

3 apples, peeled, grated
3 ripe bananas, mashed
2 teaspoons lemon juice
$\frac{1}{2}$ cup (1 stick) butter, softened
2 cups sugar
2 eggs
3 cups flour
$1\frac{1}{2}$ teaspoons baking powder
$1\frac{1}{2}$ teaspoons baking soda
1 teaspoon vanilla

🍅 Preheat oven to 350°.

🍅 Sprinkle apples and bananas with lemon juice in bowl.
In separate bowl, cream butter, sugar and eggs and
beat well. Stir in fruit.

🍅 Add flour, baking powder, baking soda, vanilla and
¼ teaspoon salt; stir well.

🍅 Pour into 2 sprayed, floured loaf pans and bake for
50 to 55 minutes or until golden brown. Bread is
done when toothpick inserted in center comes out
clean. Serves 10 to 12.

Salads, Soups & Side Dishes

Contents

California Cobb Salad

½ head lettuce, shredded or torn
½ - 1 head romaine lettuce, shredded or torn
1 boneless, skinless chicken breast half,
    cooked, sliced
6 strips bacon, cooked crisp, crumbled
2 eggs, hard-boiled, chopped
2 large tomatoes, chopped, drained
¾ cup plus 2 tablespoons crumbled Roquefort®
    cheese, divided
1 large avocado
3 green onions with tops, chopped

🍅 Mix lettuces in large salad bowl or make 6 to
   8 individual salads. Arrange chicken on top of
   greens in one area. Repeat with separate areas of
   bacon, eggs, tomatoes and ¾ cup Roquefort® cheese.

🍅 Peel and slice avocado and arrange slices in center.
   Sprinkle remaining Roquefort® and green onions
   over top. Serve with your favorite salad dressing.
   Serves 6 to 8.

*Cobb Salad was created at the Brown
Derby Restaurant in Los Angeles in 1937.
The salad became an overnight sensation.*

Baby Spinach with Strawberries and Almonds

10 - 14 ounces fresh baby spinach leaves, stemmed
1 quart fresh strawberries, halved
1 cup slivered almonds, toasted

Tear spinach leaves into smaller pieces and add strawberries and almonds on 4 to 6 individual salad plates. Refrigerate until ready to serve. Pour your favorite dressing over chilled salad. Serves 4 to 6.

VEGETABLES	CALORIES (1 cup)	VITAMINS (Top 3)	MINERALS (Top 3)
Asparagus	40	Vitamin A Vitamin C Vitamin B3	Potassium Phosphorus Calcium
Broccoli	55	Vitamin A Vitamin C Vitamin E	Potassium Phosphorus, Calcium
Carrots	55	Vitamin A Vitamin C Vitamin E	Potassium Calcium Phosphorus
Cauliflower	30	Vitamin C Vitamin A Vitamin K	Potassium Phosphorus Calcium
Green Bell Pepper	15	Vitamin C Vitamin A Vitamin K	Potassium Phosphorus Magnesium
Kale	35	Vitamin A Vitamin C Vitamin E	Potassium Phosphorus Calcium
Spinach	10	Vitamin C Vitamin A Vitamin E	Potassium Calcium Magnesium

Grilled Chicken Caesar Salad

4 boneless, skinless chicken breast halves, grilled
10 - 12 ounces romaine salad greens
½ cup shredded parmesan cheese
1 cup seasoned croutons
Bacon crumbles, optional
Cracked black pepper, optional
¾ cup Caesar or Italian dressing

- Cut chicken breasts into strips. Combine chicken, salad greens, cheese and croutons in large bowl.

- Add bacon and pepper if needed. When ready to serve, toss with dressing. Serves 4 to 6.

The original Caesar Salad was created by Caesar Cardini, an Italian immigrant and restaurant owner in San Diego. When his restaurant ran out of salad ingredients on a busy 4th of July in 1924, Cardini made a dramatic table-side presentation by tossing romaine lettuce with shredded parmesan, fresh croutons and a special dressing. It is now considered an emperor of salads.

Crunchy Coleslaw

4 cups finely shredded cabbage
½ cup chopped celery
¼ cup chopped bell pepper
¼ cup shredded carrots
1 tablespoon chopped green onion
¾ cup sour cream
¼ cup mayonnaise
3 tablespoons vinegar
3 tablespoons sugar

- Combine cabbage, celery, bell pepper, carrots and onion in bowl. In separate bowl combine sour cream, mayonnaise, vinegar, sugar, 1 teaspoon salt and ⅛ teaspoon pepper and mix well.

- Pour half of dressing over cabbage, mix lightly and refrigerate. Taste and add more dressing if needed before serving. Serves 4 to 6.

Some mistakes are too much fun to make only once.
—Anonymous

Marinated Corn Salad

3 (15 ounce) cans whole kernel corn, drained
1 red bell pepper, seeded, chopped
1 cup quartered cherry tomatoes
¾ cup chopped celery
1 (8 ounce) bottle Italian salad dressing

🍅 Combine corn, bell pepper, tomatoes and celery in bowl with lid. Pour salad dressing over vegetables.

🍅 Cover and refrigerate for several hours before serving. Serves 8 to 10.

TIP: A couple dashes of Tabasco® sauce gives this a nice little kick.

Sweet corn grown commercially has yellow kernels. Sweet corn with white kernels and "peaches-and-cream" corn with white and yellow kernels are usually found in local farmers' markets. Sweet corn should be eaten as soon after picking as possible because its sugars quickly turn to starches.

Marinated Chives-Cucumbers

1 cup vinegar
½ cup sugar
¼ cup chopped chives
Cracked black pepper
4 - 6 cucumbers, peeled

🍅 Combine vinegar, sugar, chives, cracked black pepper and ½ teaspoon salt in large measuring cup. Slice cucumbers about ⅓-inch thick and place in large bowl.

🍅 Pour marinade over cucumbers, cover and refrigerate. Serves 6 to 8.

Family meals help children learn the basics of good nutrition and how to take care of themselves. Family meals don't have to be big deals, but can be simple meals with basic nutrition. Children learn how to strive for good health and about taking responsibility for themselves. Family meals provide a time for family traditions and family memories to grow.

Tropical Mango-Spinach Salad

3 - 4 cups baby spinach leaves or spring greens
3 ripe mangoes, peeled, sliced
1 avocado, peeled, seeded, thinly sliced
$\frac{1}{4}$ - $\frac{1}{2}$ cup walnut halves, toasted
$\frac{1}{8}$ - $\frac{1}{4}$ cup balsamic vinaigrette dressing

Arrange greens on 4 individual salad plates and divide mangoes, avocado slices and walnuts evenly. Serve dressing on the side. Serves 4.

Family meals are great for finding out about your children's lives. When children talk about their day and their activities, you learn what they are learning. You can explain important points and use these times as teaching moments. It is not a time for conflict or strong discipline, but a time for love and nurturing.

Apple, Pear and Goat Cheese Salad

Fresh lemon juice
1 medium pear, cored, peeled, sliced
1 medium apple, cored, sliced
¼ cup walnut pieces
4 - 6 cups butter lettuce or mixed salad greens
¼ - ½ cup goat cheese
¼ cup walnut-flavored olive oil

🍎 Preheat oven to 225°.

🍎 Sprinkle lemon juice over pear and apple slices to prevent discoloration. Toast walnut pieces on baking sheet in oven for about 10 minutes to bring out flavors.

🍎 Combine lettuce, walnuts, cheese and oil in large bowl and toss. Divide into individual servings and arrange pear and apple slices on top. Serves 6 to 8.

TIP: Sprouts are a great addition.

A fresh apple is 25% air. That is why they float in the barrel when we "bob for apples".

Raspberry-Tomato Salad with Baby Spinach

8 - 10 ounces baby spinach, stemmed, torn
1 - 2 cups raspberries
1 cup grape tomatoes
½ cup sliced almonds, toasted
¼ cup red wine vinegar
½ teaspoon dry leaf tarragon, crushed
½ teaspoon dijon-style mustard
1 cup olive oil

● Toss spinach, raspberries, tomatoes and almonds in salad bowl and refrigerate. Mix vinegar and tarragon in small saucepan, bring to a boil and remove from heat.

● Pour mixture into bowl and blend in mustard and olive oil. Slowly pour dressing over salad, season with a little salt and pepper and toss well or serve in individual dishes. Serves 3 to 4.

The best sweetener of all is the natural sweetness of fresh fruits.

Insalata Caprese

(Salad in the style of Capri – a delicious traditional combination of tomatoes, mozzarella cheese and basil)

2 - 3 tomatoes, thickly sliced
6 - 9 thick slices fresh mozzarella cheese
1 Texas 1015 or Vidalia® sweet onion, sliced, optional
3 tablespoons extra-virgin olive oil
6 - 9 leaves fresh basil
Cracked black pepper

🍅 Arrange tomatoes, mozzarella and sweet onion slices in overlapping, alternating pattern on serving dish. Drizzle olive oil over arrangement and sprinkle with salt and pepper.

🍅 Place fresh basil leaves on top of mozzarella. Serves 4.

TIP: The addition of sweet onion makes this dish even more exceptional.

Every year since the 1940's, the town of Buñol, Spain has held La Tomatina, a tomato-throwing spectacle in its streets. People come from all over the world just for the fun of throwing more than 100 metric tons of ripe tomatoes.

Cold Strawberry Soup

2½ cups fresh strawberries
⅓ cup sugar
½ cup sour cream
½ cup whipping cream
½ cup light red wine

Place strawberries and sugar in blender and puree.
Pour into mixing bowl, stir in sour cream and cream
and blend well.

Add 1 cup water and wine. Stir well and refrigerate.
Serves 4.

*Strawberries are the most popular fruit
in the world. They have more vitamin
C than any other fruit. When kids eat
8 strawberries, they get 140% of their
daily requirement of vitamin C.*

*If all the strawberries produced in
California in one year were placed end to
end, they would circle the world 15 times.*

Incredible
Broccoli-Cheese Soup

1½ cups chopped broccoli
3 tablespoons butter
½ onion, minced
¼ cup flour
1 (16 ounce) carton half-and-half cream
2 cups chicken broth
⅛ teaspoon cayenne pepper
¼ cup minced carrot
1 (16 ounce) package cubed, mild Mexican Velveeta® cheese

● Microwave broccoli in covered bowl with several tablespoons water on HIGH for 5 minutes or until tender; rotate several times.

● Melt butter in large saucepan and cook onion until it is translucent. Add flour, stir and gradually add half-and-half cream, chicken broth, ½ teaspoon salt and ¼ teaspoon pepper, cayenne pepper and minced carrots and stir constantly.

● Heat until mixture thickens. (Do not boil.) Add cheese and stir constantly until cheese melts. Add cooked broccoli and serve hot. Serves 6.

Old-Fashioned Tomato Soup

2½ pounds fresh tomatoes, peeled, seeded, chopped
   or 4 cups canned stewed, chopped tomatoes
3 - 4 cups chicken stock
2 ribs celery, minced
1 carrot, minced
1 onion, minced
2 tablespoons basil

- In large soup pot, combine tomatoes, chicken stock, celery, carrot and onion on high heat.

- After soup begins to boil, reduce heat to low and simmer for 15 to 30 minutes. Add basil, salt and pepper to taste. Serves 6 to 8.

Researchers have found that tomatoes have a large amount of lycopene in them. Lycopene has 100 times more powerful antioxidants than vitamins E and C. The high vitamin, mineral and nutrient values of tomatoes may help slow down the aging process and some degenerative diseases such as cancers, cardiovascular disease and blindness.

Asparagus with Prosciutto

1 pound fresh asparagus, trimmed
2 tablespoons extra-virgin olive oil
¼ - ½ pound thinly sliced prosciutto
⅓ cup freshly grated parmesan cheese

- Preheat oven to 400°.

- Arrange asparagus in single layer in shallow baking dish and drizzle olive oil over asparagus. Bake uncovered about 10 minutes or until asparagus is tender.

- Wrap several stems of asparagus with slice of prosciutto.

- To serve, sprinkle with a little salt and pepper and parmesan cheese. Serves 4.

Prosciutto is very thinly sliced ham cured in specific regions of Italy and has been praised for its flavor for thousands of years. It goes especially well with asparagus, melon and mozzarella. You can find it in your grocery store deli, but it isn't a bargain item.

Fresh Asparagus with Citrus Dressing

3 tablespoons extra-virgin olive oil
⅔ cup fresh orange juice
1 teaspoon orange zest plus additional zest for garnish
2 bunches fresh asparagus, ends trimmed
1 (12 ounce) carton cherry tomatoes
½ cup toasted ground almonds
Parmesan cheese, grated or shaved

- Combine oil, orange juice, orange zest and ½ teaspoon black pepper in small bowl and mix well.

- Place about 2 cups water and ½ teaspoon salt in large skillet (large enough to lay asparagus flat in skillet) and bring to a boil.

- Add asparagus and cook until tender, about 7 to 8 minutes. Drain asparagus on cloth towel and scatter some ice cubes over asparagus to cool. Discard most of water in skillet, add tomatoes and cook until soft.

- Arrange asparagus and tomatoes on platter or individual plates. Pour dressing over asparagus and top with almonds, additional orange zest and parmesan. Serves 4 to 6.

Spicy Buttered Beets

¼ cup sugar
½ teaspoon cinnamon
¼ teaspoon ground ginger
6 - 8 medium cooked beets, peeled, sliced
¼ cup butter

🍅 Preheat oven to 350°.

🍅 Combine sugar, ¾ teaspoon salt, cinnamon and ginger. Sprinkle over beets; toss lightly to coat evenly. Scoop into sprayed ½-quart baking dish. Dot with butter.

🍅 Bake for 20 minutes or until beets heat through. Serves 6.

TIP: One way to cook beets: Wrap in foil and bake at 350° for 1 hour. Peel when cool and slice.

Beets are loaded with vitamins A, B1, B2, B6 and C. They are also excellent sources of calcium, magnesium, copper, phosphorus, sodium and iron. The amount of iron is not large, but it is of the highest quality. Beetroot and beet greens are powerful blood cleansers and builders.

Germantown Sweet-Sour Cabbage

2 - 4 slices bacon
1 medium head red cabbage, shredded
½ onion, diced
1 apple, diced
1 tablespoon vinegar
1 tablespoon sugar
1½ tablespoons flour, optional

In large skillet, fry bacon and remove from pan. With bacon drippings still in skillet, add cabbage to hot fat. Add onion and apple and stir well.

Add 2 cups water and cook on low heat for 1 hour. (Liquid should cook down in this time.)

Season with salt, pepper, vinegar and sugar. If desired, thicken by mixing flour with a little warm water and stirring it into dish. Garnish with crumbled bacon. Serves 6 to 8.

Why did the man at the orange juice factory lose his job?

He couldn't concentrate.

Brown Sugar Carrots

½ pound baby carrots, peeled, cut on the diagonal
2 tablespoons chicken or vegetable broth
¼ cup (½ stick) butter
3 tablespoons brown sugar
½ teaspoon ground ginger

🥕 Boil carrots in saucepan with enough water to cover until carrots are tender-crisp. Drain.

🥕 Combine broth with butter, brown sugar and ginger in saucepan. Heat thoroughly.

🥕 Add carrots, stirring gently, and cook for 10 minutes. Serve hot. Serves 4.

Lettuce, peas, cucumbers, tomatoes and basil are easy to grow. Lettuce and peas are cool season plants and cucumbers and tomatoes grow after temperatures reach 70° consistently.

Homestead Collard Greens

2 bunches fresh collard greens
2½ cups chicken broth
5 - 6 strips bacon
1 onion, chopped
1 red bell pepper, seeded, chopped
1 tablespoon seasoned salt
1 teaspoon seasoned black pepper
½ teaspoon sugar
1 teaspoon hot sauce, optional

● Wash and drain collard greens, cut stems off and coarsely chop greens. Place in large soup pot and cover with broth and 2 cups water.

● Fry bacon in skillet, remove from pan and crumble. In same skillet with bacon drippings, saute onion and bell pepper. Add seasoned salt, black pepper, sugar and hot sauce, if you like.

● Add onion-bell pepper mixture to soup pot and heat to a full boil. Reduce heat, cover and simmer for 1 hour. Taste for seasoning. Serves 6 to 8.

Mexican Street Corner Corn

Corn made this way was prepared by vendors on street corners in San Antonio, Texas during the early 1900's.

Fresh corn-on-the-cob in husks
Butter
Mayonnaise
Queso cotija, grated*
Lime

● Shuck each ear of corn by removing outer husks, but set aside larger husks.

● Remove all silks on corn and spread butter over corn. Season with salt and pepper and wrap corn in inner husks and large outer husks to hold butter. Tie with long pieces of outer husks. (If you prefer, cook corn without husks directly over heat.)

● Place on grill and cook 15 to 30 minutes, depending on coals and size of corn. Turn once or twice while cooking. Remove from grill.

● Spread with light coating of mayonnaise, roll in grated queso cotija and sprinkle with lime juice. Serve immediately.

*TIP: Queso cotija is a hard cheese similar to parmesan cheese. You can find it in grocery stores near the Mexican chorizo and sausages.

Bacon-Flavored Fresh String Beans

1 - 2 pounds fresh green beans, trimmed
5 - 8 green onions with tops, chopped
3 - 5 cloves garlic, minced
2 tablespoons butter
5 - 6 slices bacon, fried crisp, crumbled
½ to 1 cup toasted pine nuts, optional
Onion rings, optional

● Fill large saucepan with enough water to cover green beans. Bring to a boil and carefully place green beans in water. Cook until tender-crisp.

● Drain water from saucepan and fill with ice cold water to stop cooking and keep bright green color in green beans.

● Saute green onions and garlic in skillet with butter until garlic is translucent. Toss with green beans, bacon and pine nuts. Top with onion rings and serve immediately. Serves 4.

TIP: Fresh green beans are so good, try this lemon-butter sauce with another batch of 1 to 2 pounds green beans: ¼ to ½ cup (½ to 1 stick) butter, 1 to 2 tablespoons fresh lemon juice, 1 to 2 teaspoons olive oil and ½ to 1 cup toasted pine nuts.

Garlic Roasted Potatoes

18 - 20 small, golden potatoes with peels
½ cup (1 stick) butter, melted
¼ cup fresh snipped rosemary
2 - 4 cloves garlic, minced

Steam potatoes in large saucepan with
small amount of water until tender. (Test with fork.)

In separate saucepan, combine butter, rosemary,
garlic, 1 teaspoon salt (or sea salt) and 1 teaspoon
black pepper. Heat until ingredients mix well.

Place potatoes in serving dish, spoon butter mixture
over potatoes. Serves 6 to 8.

*Roasted garlic is one of life's rewards.
Cut the tops off a bulb or head of garlic,
arrange several bulbs (with skin) on foil in
baking pan and pour olive oil over individual
cloves in bulbs. Seal foil and roast in
oven at 350° for about 15 to 20 minutes
or until cloves are tender. Remove each
clove from bulb. Slice and add to any
dish, mash with butter or mash and use as
a spread. Enjoy!*

Unbelievable Sweet Potato Casserole

This is the best sweet potato recipe you will ever make!

4 large sweet potatoes, cooked, peeled
⅓ cup evaporated milk
¾ cup sugar
2 eggs, beaten
¼ cup (½ stick) butter, melted
1 teaspoon vanilla

- Preheat oven to 350°.

- Mash sweet potatoes in bowl, add evaporated milk, sugar, eggs, butter and vanilla, and mix well.

- Pour into sprayed 7 x 11-inch baking dish.

Topping:

1 cup packed light brown sugar
⅓ cup (⅔ stick) butter, melted
½ cup flour
1 cup chopped pecans

- Mix topping ingredients in bowl and sprinkle over casserole. Bake for 35 minutes or until crusty on top. Serves 8.

Sweet Onion Rings

*Texas 1015 SuperSweet onions were bred to be
flatter than regular round onions so that onion
rings would be more uniform in size. They were also
bred to eliminate tears when you peel and slice
them. Vidalia® onions, grown near the small city of
Vidalia, Georgia are also famous as sweet onions.*

2 large Texas 1015 SuperSweet onions
2 cups buttermilk*
1 cup seasoned breadcrumbs or cracker crumbs
1 cup cornmeal
Canola oil

- Slice onions about ¼ inch thick and drop into large
  bowl. Pour buttermilk over top and marinate for
  about 30 minutes before frying.

- In separate bowl, mix breadcrumbs, cornmeal,
  1 teaspoon salt and ½ teaspoon pepper. Dredge
  buttermilk-soaked onion rings through cornmeal
  mixture. Return to buttermilk to moisten and again
  dredge through cornmeal mixture.

Continued next page...

Continued from previous page…

- In deep saucepan or deep fryer with enough oil to cover onion rings, heat oil to 375° to 400° and drop rings into hot oil.

- Fry for about 3 minutes or until rings turn golden brown. Remove from fryer with slotted spoon and drain on paper towels. Sprinkle a little salt over top and serve immediately. Serves 6 to 8.

*TIP: To make buttermilk, mix 1 cup milk with
        1 tablespoon lemon juice or vinegar and let
        stand for about 10 minutes.*

The USDA suggests that adults eat at least 3 cups of leafy green vegetables per week. People who eat greater amounts of vegetables have higher energy levels and feel less lethargic and stressed. Fresh green vegetables help prevent heart disease and stroke, cataracts, high blood pressure, cancer, macular degeneration and obesity.

Creamy Squash

6 - 8 medium yellow squash
1 (8 ounce) package cream cheese, cubed, softened
2 tablespoons butter
½ teaspoon sugar

- Cut squash in little pieces and place in large saucepan. Cover with water and boil for 10 to 15 minutes or until tender. Drain.

- Add cream cheese, butter, sugar, and ¾ teaspoon each of salt and pepper to squash.

- Cook over low heat and stir until cream cheese melts. Serve hot. Serves 8.

The word "squash" is adapted from the Narragansett Indian word "askutasquash". Squash has been farmed as a crop in the Americas for at least 10,000 years.

Zucchini Patties

1 pound (about 3) zucchini squash with peel, grated
1 tablespoon minced fresh parsley
1 teaspoon minced fresh chives
1 cup buttermilk pancake mix
1 egg, beaten
⅓ cup oil

● Combine zucchini, parsley, chives, pancake mix, egg, and ¼ teaspoon each of salt and pepper, stirring well.

● Drop tablespoonfuls of mixture in hot oil (375°). Flatten with spatula and cook until golden brown, turning once. Drain on paper towel. Serve immediately. Serves 6.

According to the U.S. Department of Agriculture teenage girls need three servings of fruit and four servings of vegetables. Teenage boys need four servings of fruit and five servings of vegetables. Active men and women need three servings of fruit and four servings of vegetables.

Small children and inactive adults need two servings of fruit and three servings of vegetables.

Fried Zucchini
or Yellow Squash

This is incredibly good!

3 large zucchini or yellow squash, sliced
Cornmeal
Flour
Canola oil

- Salt and pepper zucchini on both sides. Dip each slice into shallow bowl with twice as much cornmeal as flour.

- Drop into hot oil in large skillet over medium high heat and cook until brown on each side. Flip each after a few minutes. Serves 4 to 6.

Middle age is when you choose your cereal for the fiber, not the toy.

Parmesan Broiled Veggies

Change this recipe for the vegetables you have on hand.

Tomatoes
Zucchini
Summer squash
Bell peppers
Eggplant
Butter, melted
Parmesan cheese, freshly grated
Breadcrumbs

● Slice vegetables of choice about ½ inch thick. Place in sprayed 9 x 13-inch baking pan. Sprinkle with a little salt and pepper.

● Mix butter, parmesan and small portion of breadcrumbs in bowl to paste consistency. (Use more parmesan than breadcrumbs.) Spread over slices of vegetables. Place on top rack under broiler until cheese mixture bubbles and browns a little.

> *It's bizarre that the produce man is more important to my children's health than the pediatrician.*
> —Meryl Streep

Grilled Vegetables with Cilantro-Lime Butter

½ cup (1 stick) butter
¼ - ½ cup chopped cilantro
2 tablespoons lime juice
½ teaspoon hot sauce, optional
Fresh vegetables (tomatoes, onions, zucchini, summer
    squash, mushrooms, bell pepper, corn, eggplant, etc.)
Olive oil

● Melt butter with cilantro, lime juice and hot sauce in
saucepan. Rub vegetables of choice with a little olive
oil and place on skewer or grill rack.

● Dip brush (or cloth wrapped over spoon) into butter
sauce and baste vegetables generously while they cook.

● When grill marks show and vegetables are tender,
remove from grill and place in serving dish. Pour
remaining butter sauce over top before serving.
Makes about 1 cup sauce.

*Let your food be your medicine and your
medicine be your food.*
                                        -Hippocrates

Quick Caponata

*This Italian accompaniment is a great side dish
or chunky dip. It is especially good with seafood.*

1 cup minced celery
¾ cup minced onion
1 small eggplant with peel, cubed
3 - 4 tomatoes, cubed
¼ cup red wine vinegar
1½ teaspoons olive oil
1 (4 ounce) can sliced ripe olives, drained

Combine celery, onion and 1 tablespoon water in bowl
and microwave on HIGH about 90 seconds, stir and
microwave again for about 90 seconds or until tender.

Microwave eggplant cubes in 2 tablespoons water on
HIGH for about 3 minutes, stir well and microwave
for about 2 more minutes or until tender.

Combine tomatoes, vinegar, oil, ½ teaspoon salt
and pepper to taste in skillet. Cook for about
3 to 4 minutes over medium heat until tender.

Add rest of vegetables and olives and simmer
uncovered until most liquid evaporates, about
10 minutes. Serves about 8 to 10.

Cheesy Vegetable Casserole

3 cups chopped mixed vegetables
1¾ cups shredded American cheese
¾ cup mayonnaise
1 tube round, buttery crackers, crushed
6 tablespoons (¾ stick) butter, melted

🍅 Preheat oven to 350°.

🍅 Cook vegetables in saucepan with a little water, bring
to a boil and cook until slightly tender. Drain and
place in sprayed 2-quart baking dish.

🍅 Mix cheese and mayonnaise in bowl and spread over
vegetables. In separate bowl, combine cracker crumbs
and butter and sprinkle on top. Bake for 35 minutes.
Serves 8.

*People who eat raw foods usually have
more energy, stamina and are better
able to fight health problems. Most
people who eat raw foods sleep better,
think more clearly and go through their
days more happily.*

Main Dishes

Veggie
Beef
Chicken
Seafood

Contents

Spinach-Feta Cheese Pizza

1 tablespoon olive oil
2 cloves garlic, peeled, minced, divided
½ red onion or 2 fresh green onions, minced
1 (12 inch) prepared pizza crust
1 (10 ounce) package fresh spinach, chopped
1½ cups shredded mozzarella cheese
1 red bell pepper, seeded, julienned
1 (4 ounce) package crumbled feta cheese

🍅 Preheat oven to 400°.

🍅 Mix oil, 1 clove garlic and onions in small, microwave-safe bowl and microwave on HIGH for 30 seconds. Prepare pizza crust by rubbing garlic mixture over surface of crust.

🍅 Spread spinach evenly over crust. Sprinkle mozzarella cheese evenly over spinach.

🍅 Spread bell pepper strips evenly over mozzarella cheese. Sprinkle with a little salt and pepper and top with feta cheese.

🍅 Bake for about 10 minutes or until cheese melts and crust is golden brown. Let stand 5 minutes before cutting into slices to serve. Serves 2 to 4.

Pasta Primavera

The Italian term primavera *means spring style and indicates the addition of fresh vegetables to a dish.*

6 ounces bowtie pasta
1½ cups vegetable broth
1 cup sliced baby carrots
1 cup sliced red bell pepper
1 cup fresh snap peas
1 cup (about 6) fresh asparagus spears, cut in 1-inch
  diagonal pieces
1 cup grated parmesan cheese
1 cup half-and-half cream

🍅 Prepare pasta according to package directions and drain.

🍅 Bring broth to a boil in large skillet. Lower heat,
add carrots, bell pepper and peas and cook about
10 minutes. Add asparagus and cook about 5 minutes.
Drain liquid and add pasta.

🍅 In saucepan, combine parmesan cheese, half-and-half
cream, and dash of salt and pepper. Cook on low-
medium heat until hot. Pour over pasta and vegetables
and mix well. Serves 6 to 8.

Grilled Portobello Burgers

4 large portobello mushroom caps
Fat-free balsamic vinaigrette dressing
4 multi-grain hamburger buns, toasted
Burger "fixin's" (lettuce, tomato slices, onion rings, etc.)

● Preheat gas grill to medium heat or prepare charcoal grill. Brush mushroom caps with dressing and season to taste with salt and freshly ground black pepper.

● Grill, turning once, about 10 minutes or until soft (do not overcook or you will lose all the natural juices).

● Place mushrooms on toasted buns and add "fixin's". Drizzle with dressing and serve. Serves 4.

TIP: Swiss cheese is a great addition.

How does a ghost eat an apple?

By goblin it!

Short-Cut Meat Sauce with Spaghetti

1 (12 ounce) package spaghetti pasta
1 tablespoon olive oil
1 pound lean ground beef
3 small zucchini, cubed
1 onion, chopped
1 green bell pepper, seeded, chopped
2 large carrots, sliced
1 teaspoon minced garlic
1 (26 ounce) can chunky garden pasta sauce
½ cup grated parmesan cheese

Cook spaghetti in saucepan according to package directions; drain, cover and keep warm.

Heat oil in large skillet, cook beef for about 5 minutes and stir well to crumble. Stir in zucchini, onion, bell pepper, carrots, garlic, and a little salt and pepper. Stir occasionally and cook for 10 minutes or until vegetables are tender-crisp and beef is brown.

Continued next page...

Continued from previous page...

- Stir in pasta sauce, bring to a boil; reduce heat, simmer about 8 minutes and stir often.

- Place warm spaghetti on serving platter, spoon meat sauce over top and sprinkle with parmesan cheese. Serves 8 to 10.

Pasta has been around for thousands of years, but the variety and sizes we have today were made possible by mechanization. Tomato sauce, for instance, was not introduced until the 1700's and was not used in traditional Italian pasta dishes before that time.

Spaghetti and meatballs is a relatively new creation brought to America with the influx of Italian immigrants in the late 1800's.

Thomas Jefferson was the first notable American to use a pasta press, but Italian immigrants gave us the wonderful flavors in traditional Italian dishes.

Marinated Beef and Veggie Kebabs

You will not believe how good this is and how impressive it looks. It is a real treat!

2 - 2½ pounds sirloin steak
Large fresh mushrooms
Green, red and yellow bell peppers
Small onions
Cherry tomatoes
Zucchini

● Cut meat into 1½ to 2-inch pieces and quarter bell peppers. Halve onions and cherry tomatoes. Slice zucchini.

Marinade:

1 cup red wine
2 teaspoons Worcestershire sauce
2 teaspoons garlic powder
1 cup canola oil
¼ cup ketchup
2 teaspoons sugar
2 tablespoons vinegar
1 teaspoon marjoram
1 teaspoon rosemary
½ teaspoon seasoned pepper

● Mix all marinade ingredients and 1 teaspoon salt in bowl and stir well. Marinate steak for 3 to 4 hours.

Continued next page...

Continued from previous page...

- Alternate meat, mushrooms, bell peppers, onions, cherry tomatoes and zucchini on skewers.

- Cook on charcoal grill, turn on all sides. Discard uncooked marinade. Serves 8.

Marinating meats helps keep meat moist, adds flavor and tenderizes meat before grilling or cooking. Basic ingredients usually include vegetable oil (not olive oil because it solidifies when refrigerated), seasonings and acid in the form of citrus juice or vinegar.

Beef and pork aren't porous enough for marinades to penetrate very far into the meat and are sometimes marinated overnight. Chicken and turkey are more porous and do not need to be soaked for a long time. Fish soaks up marinades quickly and thoroughly; marinades should be used sparingly with seafood.

Basting sauces are used to keep meats moist, add flavor and tenderize to some degree while meats are cooking. They also help to add a brown, crispy glaze to meats. Any sauces with sugar may cause charring and burning and should be used toward the end of cooking.

Fresh Chicken Tacos

2 cups cooked, sliced chicken
1 - 2 tablespoons snipped cilantro
1 (12 ounce) package shredded cheddar cheese, divided
14 - 16 tortillas or taco shells
2 - 3 tomatoes, chopped, drained
1 large onion, chopped
1 - 2 cups shredded romaine lettuce
Salsa

Stir chicken, cilantro and half of cheese together gently and warm in oven at 250° to 300° just enough for cheese to melt a little.

Warm tortillas in lightly damp paper towels for 20 seconds in microwave. Or, fry tortillas, one at a time, in hot oil for about 5 seconds on one side and fold in half.

Hold tortilla open about 1 inch for several seconds more. Turn and cook just long enough for tortilla to hold its shape. Drain and arrange side by side.

Serve immediately with chicken, tomatoes, onion, lettuce, salsa and remaining cheese. Serves 6 to 8.

Homer's Best Basted Chicken

4 - 6 chicken breast halves
Seasoned pepper or fresh cracked black pepper
½ cup (1 stick) butter
2 teaspoons Worcestershire sauce
2 dashes hot sauce
2 tablespoons lemon juice
½ teaspoon garlic salt
1 (12 ounce) can lemon-lime soda

Sprinkle chicken breasts with seasoned pepper and leave at room temperature for 30 minutes.

Melt butter in saucepan with Worcestershire, hot sauce, lemon juice and garlic salt. Add lemon-lime soda. Set aside ¼ cup mixture.

Cook chicken in smoker or over grill with charcoal and mesquite-wood fire. Cook over medium-low heat, turn often and baste frequently with butter-lemon mixture.

(Do not cook too fast or too long or chicken will become dry.) When meat is no longer pink, remove from heat and pour remaining butter-lemon sauce over chicken to keep it moist. Serves 4 to 6.

Bayou Killer Shrimp

*All the spices make this recipe an all-time
Cajun favorite!*

2 tablespoons garlic powder
2 tablespoons onion powder
2 tablespoons chili powder
1 - 2 teaspoons cayenne pepper
3 - 4 lemons, quartered
4 - 5 pounds medium shrimp, shelled, cleaned
Bell peppers, onion, zucchini, tomatoes

🍅 Mix garlic powder, onion powder, chili powder,
cayenne, and 1 tablespoon each of salt and pepper in
small bowl or shaker.

🍅 Squeeze a little lemon juice over shrimp. Sprinkle
generously with seasoning mixture and place on
skewers with vegetable pieces.

🍅 Grill over medium-low fire and turn once or twice
until done. Serve immediately with remaining lemon.
Serves 4.

Grilled Garlic Shrimp

¼ cup (½ stick) butter
1 heaping teaspoon minced garlic
1 teaspoon dried parsley
¼ cup dry white wine
1 pound medium fresh or frozen shrimp, peeled, veined

● Combine all ingredients except shrimp in saucepan; add about ½ teaspoon pepper. Cook sauce mixture for about 1 minute.

● Thread shrimp onto metal skewers and grill on uncovered grill directly over medium-hot coals for about 12 minutes or until pink. Brush shrimp frequently with sauce. Serves 4.

TIP: Rub a little olive oil on asparagus, corn-on-the-cob, tomatoes and zucchini slices and cook them right on the grill with the shrimp. Cleanup is easy and this creates a beautiful plate.

Americans eat more than 1 billion pounds of shrimp every year.

Sweets
Cakes
Ice Cream Treats
Fruits
Pies & Cobbler

Contents

Sweet Carrot Cake

2 cups flour, sifted
2 cups sugar
1 teaspoon baking powder
1 teaspoon baking soda
1 teaspoon ground cinnamon
4 eggs
1½ cups vegetable oil
2 cups grated carrots

Preheat oven to 350°.

Sift ¼ teaspoon salt and dry ingredients in mixing bowl.

In separate bowl, blend eggs and vegetable oil. Add dry ingredients and mix thoroughly. Stir in carrots.

Continued next page...

Carrots are the sweetest vegetable except sugar beets. Because carrots were so readily available, peasants in the Middle Ages made sweet cakes out of carrots. During World War II, Britain's rationing of sugar made carrot cakes a standard. During the 1960's in the U.S. carrot cake was a fad. Today it is a favorite dessert with cream cheese icing, white icing or a glaze.

Continued from previous page...

Pour into 3 sprayed, floured 9-inch layer cake pans and bake for 30 to 40 minutes.

Frosting for Carrot Cake:

1 (8 ounce) package cream cheese, softened
½ cup (1 stick) butter
1 teaspoon vanilla
1 (16 ounce) package powdered sugar
1 cup chopped pecans, optional

Beat cream cheese and butter in bowl. Add vanilla and powdered sugar. Frost layers and stack; frost top and sides of cake. Sprinkle with pecans. Serves 10 to 12.

How many times during our childhoods did we hear the adage "An apple a day keeps the doctor away"? As it turns out, the truth is apples are a very nutritious food. They contain Vitamin C plus many other antioxidants, which are cancer fighters.

The Best Fresh Apple Cake

1½ cups canola oil
2 cups sugar
3 eggs
2½ cups sifted flour
½ teaspoon baking soda
2 teaspoons baking powder
½ teaspoon ground cinnamon
1 teaspoon vanilla
3 cups peeled, grated apples
1 cup chopped pecans

● Preheat oven to 350°.

● Mix oil, sugar and eggs in bowl and beat well.

● In separate bowl, combine flour, ½ teaspoon salt, baking soda, baking powder and cinnamon. Gradually add flour mixture to creamed mixture.

● Add vanilla, fold in apples and pecans and pour into sprayed, floured tube pan.

Continued from previous page...

🍎 Bake for 1 hour. While cake is still warm, invert onto serving plate.

Glaze:

2 tablespoons butter, melted
2 tablespoons milk
1 cup powdered sugar
1 teaspoon vanilla
¼ teaspoon lemon extract

🍎 Combine and mix all ingredients in bowl and drizzle over cake while cake is still warm. Serves 18 to 20.

Apples are more efficient than caffeine at waking you up in the morning.

It's better to find a whole worm in your apple than it is to find half a worm.

Strawberry Trifle

1 (5 ounce) package French vanilla instant pudding mix
1 (10 ounce) loaf pound cake or angel food cake
½ cup sherry, divided
2 cups fresh strawberries, sliced
Frozen whipped topping, thawed

● Prepare pudding according to package directions.

● Layer half pound cake slices in bottom of 8-inch glass
  bowl. Sprinkle with ¼ cup sherry. Add layer of half
  strawberries. Next, layer half pudding.

● Repeat these layers. Refrigerate overnight or several
  hours.

● Before serving, top with whipped topping. Serves 4.

TIP: *Individual servings in parfait or wine glasses create*
    a beautiful dessert.

*About 94% of all American households
eat strawberries. California produces over
one billion pounds of strawberries annually,
about 75% of all the strawberries eaten in
the U.S.*

Homemade Peach Ice Cream

1½ quarts mashed, ripe peaches
2 tablespoons vanilla
2 (14 ounce) cans sweetened condensed milk
1 (12 ounce) can evaporated milk
½ cup sugar
½ gallon milk

● Combine peaches, vanilla, ½ teaspoon salt, sweetened condensed milk, evaporated milk and sugar in ice cream freezer container and mix well. Add milk to mixture line in container.

● Freeze according to manufacturer's directions. Serves 10 to 12.

Some form of ice cream has been around as far back as 2000 BC in China. It didn't really become popular in the U.S. until the 1850's after Nancy Johnson invented the hand crank ice cream freezer. The first commercial ice cream freezer didn't appear until the 1920's.

Ice Cream with Hot Raspberry Sauce

2 pints fresh raspberries
¾ cup sugar
2 tablespoons cornstarch
Ice cream

Soak raspberries with sugar in ½ cup water in saucepan for about 20 minutes. Pour small amount of water from raspberries into small cup. Add cornstarch and stir well to dissolve cornstarch.

Pour raspberries and cornstarch mixture into blender and process to desired consistency. Strain over saucepan. (Discard seeds and pulp.)

Bring to a boil, reduce heat to low and cook for 2 to 4 minutes or until sauce thickens; stir constantly. Serve over ice cream. Serves 4.

"Brain freeze" was invented in 1994 by 7-Eleven® to explain the pain one feels when drinking a Slurpee too fast. The medical term is sphenopalatine ganglioneuralgia. It's also called ice cream headache.

Honey Baked Pears

6 medium pears, cored, halved lengthwise
¾ cup honey
2 tablespoons crystallized ginger, finely chopped

🍅 Preheat oven to 350°.

🍅 Place cut pears in sprayed 9 x 13-inch baking pan. Drizzle with honey and sprinkle with finely chopped ginger and add ¾ cup water.

🍅 Cover and bake for 40 minutes. Serves 6.

A group of chess players checked into a hotel and talked to each other in the lobby about a tournament victory. After some time, the hotel manager asked them to leave the lobby. "Why?" asked one of the players. "Because", he said, "I don't like a bunch of chess nuts boasting in an open foyer."

Kahlua Fruit Dip

1 (8 ounce) package cream cheese, softened
1 (8 ounce) carton whipped topping
⅔ cup packed brown sugar
⅓ cup Kahlua® liqueur
1 (8 ounce) carton sour cream
Sliced fresh fruit

Whip cream cheese in bowl until creamy and fold in whipped topping.

Add brown sugar, Kahlua® liqueur and sour cream and mix well.

Refrigerate for 24 hours before serving with fresh fruit. Makes 3 cups.

You can't change the past, but you can ruin the present by worrying over the future.

–Anonymous

Cookie Crust Fruit Pizza

What a way to get your daily fruit servings!
Party perfect!

1 (16 ounce) package refrigerated sugar cookie dough
1 (8 ounce) package reduced-fat cream cheese
1 cup sugar, divided
2 teaspoons vanilla
4 cups seasonal fruit, sliced or cut into bite-size pieces
3 tablespoons cornstarch
1 cup fresh orange or pineapple juice

🍒 Press cookie dough into circle on 12-inch pizza pan. Bake according to package directions. Cool.

🍒 Combine cream cheese, ½ cup sugar and vanilla in mixing bowl and beat until smooth. Spread evenly over cookie crust. Arrange fruit on top of cream cheese mixture.

🍒 Combine remaining sugar, cornstarch and juice in 1-quart saucepan and cook over medium heat. Stir until sugar mixture boils and thickens. Cool and spread over fruit. Cut into 8 wedges. Serves 8.

TIP: *Use raspberries, blueberries, sliced strawberries, sliced kiwi fruit, sliced bananas, sliced peaches or drained pineapple tidbits. Use toasted macadamia nuts to add crunchiness and great flavor.*

"As American as Apple Pie" *is a very familiar phrase and references apples as a symbol of America. The fact is apples are not native to America nor is apple pie an American invention.*

The apple came to the New World by way of European settlers who colonized the new land. Apples became so plentiful that they were served in some fashion at almost every meal during the colonial period.

When America became the world's largest producer of apples, the apple became universally accepted as a symbol of America and what can be accomplished.

Old-Fashioned Apple Pie

The best way to save time with this apple pie is to buy 1 (15 ounce) package refrigerated double piecrusts. Modern conveniences are good to have around.

Piecrust:

2 cups flour
$\frac{2}{3}$ cup shortening

🍅 Combine flour and 1 teaspoon salt in large bowl. Add shortening a little at a time and stir until lumps are small.

🍅 Slowly pour in 3 tablespoons cold water and stir until it mixes well. Divide dough into 2 pieces and place on floured countertop.

🍅 Roll out each piece of dough to about ⅛-inch thick. Place 1 inside 9-inch pie pan. Save remaining half for upper crust.

Continued next page...

I totally take back all those times I didn't want to take a nap when I was younger.

Continued from previous page...

Pie Filling:

2 tablespoons lemon juice
6 cups peeled, cored, sliced Gala apples
1 cup plus 1 tablespoon sugar
2 tablespoons flour
1½ teaspoons ground cinnamon

Preheat oven to 425°.

Sprinkle lemon juice over apples and stir to mix with all slices in bowl.

In separate bowl, mix sugar, flour and cinnamon. Pour over apples and stir in.

Pour pie filling into piecrust. Place second piecrust over top and seal edges of piecrusts.

Cut slits in top piecrust. Bake for 60 minutes and cool before serving. Serves 8.

The average American eats about 50 pounds of apples every year. About one-third of this total is fresh whole apples; the rest is in prepared foods such as applesauce, apple pie and other desserts, apple juice and apple cider, etc.

Easy Peach Cobbler

½ cup (1 stick) butter, melted
1 cup flour
2¼ cups sugar, divided
2 teaspoons baking powder
1 cup milk
3 - 4 cups fresh, ripe sliced peaches
1 teaspoon ground cinnamon

● Preheat oven to 350°.

● Combine butter, flour, 1 cup sugar, baking powder and
   ¼ teaspoon salt in bowl; mix in milk and blend well.

● Spoon into sprayed 9 x 13-inch glass baking dish.
   Combine sliced peaches, 1¼ cups sugar and cinnamon
   and pour over dough.

● Bake for 1 hour. Crust will come to top. Mix
   cinnamon with a little sugar and dust cobbler with
   mixture. Serves 10.

*The world's largest peach cobbler is
made every year in Georgia. It is 11 feet
long and 5 feet wide. Georgia's nickname
is the Peach State.*

Rhubarb Pie

3 cups rhubarb (about 1 pound)
2 (9-inch) refrigerated piecrusts
1 cup sugar
2 tablespoons flour
2 eggs, beaten

🍅 Preheat oven to 425°.

🍅 Peel rhubarb and cut in ½-inch pieces before measuring. Line a pie pan with 1 piecrust.

🍅 Mix sugar, flour, ⅛ teaspoon salt and eggs. Add to the rhubarb and turn into pie pan. Moisten edge of pastry with water. Cover with top crust. Press edges together and trim. Make slits in top to let steam escape.

🍅 Bake for 10 minutes. Reduce heat to 325° and continue baking for additional 30 minutes. Serves 6 to 8.

In the 1800's the first bakery was started on the yeast coast.

Homemade Preserves

No Pressure Cooker Canning

Jellies, Jams, Preserves, Marmalades, Butters & Fruits

Pickled Vegetables, Relishes & Chow-Chows

Salsa, Sauces & Juice

by Helen Hughes Hawkins

Preserving Without a Pressure Cooker

The last time I saw my mother with a pressure cooker was the day it exploded. Canning went out with a bang in our household, but canning is safer and easier today. You don't have to use a pressure cooker to preserve all fruits and vegetables.

Although it takes a little time, preserving food today takes less than half the time it used to take and you don't need as much equipment or effort. That's a pretty good deal for the rewards you get.

Equipment

- Water canner with rack for jars*

- Tongs to lift jars

- Wide-mouth canning jars for whole fruits and vegetables

- Regular canning jars for salsas, sliced fruits and vegetables

- Rubber seal lids and screw-on rings

- Towels

- Large saucepan or soup pot

- Big spoon

TIP: *You don't have to have a large, flat-bottom water canner with rack to preserve foods, but because it is made for this purpose, it is easier to add and to remove jars with the rack that comes with the canner.*

If using a soup pot, be sure to put a towel in the bottom to set jars on so they won't crack. Also be sure to leave 1 to 2 inches between jars so the boiling water can circulate around them.

Sterilizing Jars and Lids

Sterilize all jars in the dishwasher or boiling water just before using. Air dry thoroughly before adding food. Make sure there are no chips, cracks or nicks in the glass or on the rims.

Sterilize rubber seal lids in simmering water and dry just before placing on the jars.

Boiling Water Bath Method

Instead of using a pressure cooker, you can preserve food packed in jars by placing them in a boiling water bath.

1. Place jars with lids in rack of water canner and place inside canner. Fill canner with water to 1 to 2 inches above tops of jars and remove rack with jars. Mark

water line after rack is removed. This is amount of water needed to cover jars after they have been filled. Heat water to boiling. (It will take longer than you expect.)

2. Sterilize jars in boiling water in canner or in dishwasher and dry just before filling.

3. Fill hot jars with food and wipe rims clean. Tap jar on counter or press food down to remove all air bubbles. Loosely tighten rubber seal and screw-on ring.

4. Place in rack so that jars do not touch and water can circulate around the jars. Bring to a rolling boil, place lid on water canner and boil for the specified time.

(Add more boiling water if needed to make sure there is at least 1 inch above the jars. If boiling stops while processing, turn heat to highest setting and bring to a boil. Start timing again from the beginning.)

All boiling times for water baths are for elevations at sea level to 1000 feet. Increase times at higher elevations. (See chart on next page.)

Altitude (feet)	Increasing Processing Time
1,000 - 3,000	Add 5 minutes to processing time
3,001 - 6,000	Add 10 minutes to processing time
6,001 - 8,000	Add 15 minutes to processing time
8,001 - 10,000	Add 20 minutes to processing time

5. Remove canner from heat and remove jars to towels on counter with at least 1 inch of space between them.

6. Let jars cool for about 24 hours. Test to make sure the seal is good on the jar. Press lid down; if it moves up and down, it is not sealed and contents should be refrigerated and used within a few days.

7. Label sealed jars with date and contents; use within 1 year.

What Foods Can Be Preserved with the Boiling Water Bath Method?

All high acid foods, such as most tomatoes, fruits, pickles, sauerkraut, jams, jellies and fruit butters can be preserved using the water bath method because the acidity or pH of these foods is lower than 4.6. Boiling water is enough to kill bacteria, molds, yeasts in most of these foods.

Important Notes

- Mason jars and screw-on rings can be washed and reused for years. Lids with the rubber seal cannot be reused because they will not seal properly a second time.

- Use canning (Mason) jars, not mayonnaise jars or other types. Canning jars are made of specially tempered glass to withstand the high temperatures needed for processing. Common brands of Mason jars include Kerr® and Ball®.

- Canner pot must have flat bottom and sit in center of heat source. Pot should not extend more than 4 inches past the heat source.

- Pickling salt (also called canning salt) is used throughout the recipes. It is fine-grained for easy dissolving and has no additives that can discolor preserved foods.

When Ready to Use the Product

Always recheck the seal when you are ready to use the product and refrigerate contents after opening. To check the seal, press the middle of the lid and if it springs back when released, discard the contents of the jar.

How Much Food to Buy for Preserving

(All amounts are approximate.)

Food	Amount	Canned Yields
Apples	8 medium apples (2¼ pounds)	1 (9 inch) pie or 3 cups applesauce
	2 large (1 pound)	3 cups sliced (1½ pints)
Apricots	1 pound	1 pint halved
Asparagus	3 - 4 pounds	1 quart stalks
Beets	3 pounds	1 quart whole
Berries (medium size)	1 pint	1 pint whole
Blueberries	1 pound	1 - 1½ pints
	3 pounds	1 quart
Cabbage	1 head (2 pounds)	8 cups, shredded (2 quarts)
Cherries	1 quart	1 quart with pits
Cucumbers	1 pound	1 - 1½ pints
Grapes	2 quarts	1 quart jelly
Green beans	1 pound	1 pint trimmed
Okra	1 pound	1 pint sliced
Onions	1 pound	1 pint chopped
Oranges	1 pound	1 cup juice or ½ pint sections

Continued next page…

Continued from previous page...

Food	Amount	Canned Yields
Peaches	1 pound	1 pint pureed or 1 - 1½ pints sliced
Pears	1 pound	1 pint
Peppers, sweet (bell)	1 pound	1½ - 2 pints chopped
Plums	2 pounds	1 quart
Strawberries	1 pint	1 pint whole or ½ pint pureed
	1 quart	1 pint pureed
Tomatoes	1 pound	½ - 1 pint peeled, chopped
	2 - 3 pounds	1 quart peeled, chopped

Two-piece lids as shown above are the best for long-term storage. Jars that are not sealed must be refrigerated.

Conversions by Volume

Amount	Converts to:
1 Gallon	4 quarts
	8 pints
1 Quart	2 pints
1 Pint	2 cups (16 fluid ounces)

Please note: Some photographs show products after they have been moved into serving jars or have lids other than proper sealing lids recommended for preserving. Any preserves not using proper canning jars and lids that seal must be refrigerated.

Basic Fruit Syrups

Light Syrup:

🍎 Light syrup is used for small, soft fruits such as berries.

🍎 Mix 1 cup sugar with 3 cups water and bring to a gentle boil; remove from heat and use while still very hot.

Medium Syrup:

🍎 Medium syrup is used with peaches, apples, pears and sour or tart berries.

🍎 Mix 1 cup sugar with 2 cups water and bring to a gentle boil; remove from heat and use while still very hot.

Heavy Syrup:

🍎 Heavy syrup is used with sour or tart fruit – or if you want extra sweetness.

🍎 Mix 1 cup sugar with 1 cup water and bring to a gentle boil; remove from heat and use while still very hot.

Jellies, Jams, Preserves, Marmalades, Butters & Fruit

Contents

Apple Jelly

5 pounds apples, sliced
9 cups sugar
1 (32 ounce) and 1 (16 ounce) bottles apple juice
1 (1.7 ounce) box dry fruit pectin
1 teaspoon butter

🍅 Place apples in large saucepan with about 5 cups water and bring to a boil. Cover and simmer for about 15 minutes. Strain and mash apples through sieve or cheesecloth to separate peels, cores and seeds.

🍅 Place strained apples in saucepan with remaining ingredients and bring to a rolling boil. Cook for 1½ minutes and pour into hot sterilized jars* to within ½ inch of top, wipe rims clean and screw on lids.

🍅 Place jars in water bath** to cover and heat in boiling water for at least 10 minutes. Cool before tightening lids completely. Makes about 24 pints.

*Page 163: Instructions for sterilizing jars and lids.
**Page 163-165: Instructions for water bath.

Very Berry Jellies

Almost any berry will work with this recipe – so enjoy.

2 - 3 (1 quart) cartons ripe berries
3 cups sugar

Remove stems or leaves from berries and wash. Crush berries in large pot, add ¾ cup water and bring to a boil; stir frequently. Simmer for 5 minutes or until berries are soft.

Let juice from berries drip through sieve or cheesecloth, but do not mash. (Jelly will be cloudy if berries are mashed.) When you have 4 cups juice, discard cheesecloth and pulp and pour into large pot.

Add sugar, bring to rolling boil and cook until mixture flows in sheets from metal spoon. Skim foam from top and pour into hot sterilized jars* to within ½ inch of top, wipe rims clean and screw on lids.

Place jars in water bath** to cover and heat in boiling water for at least 10 minutes. Cool before tightening lids completely. Makes about 3 to 4 pints.

*Page 163: Instructions for sterilizing jars and lids.
**Page 163-165: Instructions for water bath.

Homemade Cherry Jelly

6 - 6½ pounds cherries
1 (1.7 ounce) box fruit pectin
7 cups sugar

Remove pits and puree enough cherries to equal
5 cups strained juice. Pour into saucepan with pectin
and bring to rolling boil. Add sugar, bring back to a
boil and cook for 1 to 1½ minutes.

Pour into hot sterilized jars* to within ½ inch of top,
wipe rims clean and screw on lids.

Place jars in water bath** to cover and heat in boiling
water for at least 10 minutes. Cool before tightening
lids completely. Makes about 9 to 10 pints.

*Page 163: Instructions for sterilizing jars and lids.
**Page 163-165: Instructions for water bath.

*Never recycle jars from prepared
foods (like mayonnaise or barbecue sauce,
etc.) for canning because the glass will
not withstand the temperatures used
in canning. Only use jars, lids and
seals made for canning. Never reuse
rubber seals.*

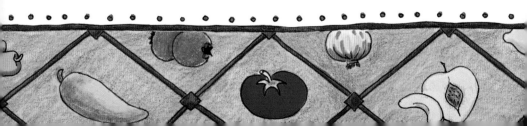

Great Granny's Corncob Jelly

These red cobs make a pretty jelly.

12 red feeder corncobs, kernels stripped
1 (1.7 ounce) package dry fruit pectin
4 cups sugar

🍎 Boil cobs in enough water to cover over medium high heat for about 20 minutes. Strain 3 cups liquid into large saucepan. Stir in pectin, bring to a boil and cook until mixture thickens.

🍎 Add sugar and bring back to a boil for 1 minute. Pour into hot sterilized jars* to within ½ inch of top, wipe rims clean and screw on lids.

🍎 Place jars in water bath** to cover and heat in boiling water for at least 10 minutes. Cool before tightening lids completely. Makes about 6 pints.

*Page 163: Instructions for sterilizing jars and lids.
**Page 163-165: Instructions for water bath.

*Grandma's granddaughter's secret:
Wash and dry jars in dishwasher before
filling with food. It's easier than washing
in boiling water by hand.*

Homemade Grape Jelly

4 - 5 pounds very ripe seedless grapes
1 (1.7 ounce) box fruit pectin
7 cups sugar

🍇 Mash enough grapes through sieve to equal 5 cups
strained juice. (Add water if needed to make 5 cups.*)
Pour into saucepan with pectin and bring to rolling
boil. Add sugar, bring back to a boil and cook for 1 to
1½ minutes.

🍇 Pour into hot sterilized jars** to within ½ inch of top,
wipe rims clean and screw on lids.

🍇 Place jars in water bath*** to cover and heat in
boiling water for at least 10 minutes. Cool before
tightening lids completely. Makes about 4 to 5 pints.

*TIP: *Very ripe grapes will make plenty of juice. Add no
more than 1 cup water if necessary.*

**Page 163: Instructions for sterilizing jars and lids.
***Page 163-165: Instructions for water bath.

Fun Jalapeno Jelly

*Great poured over cream cheese and served with
crackers! It's terrific with all meats as well.*

3 - 4 large jalapenos
3 small bell peppers, cored, seeded
1¼ cups vinegar
1 (1.7 ounce) package dry fruit pectin
5 cups sugar

Wear rubber gloves to stem, seed and mince enough
jalapenos to equal ¾ cup and enough bell peppers to
equal ¾ cup grated.

Mix jalapenos, bell peppers, vinegar, pectin and
1¼ cups water in saucepan and bring to a rolling boil.
Cook for 2 minutes at a rolling boil that cannot be
stirred down. Add sugar and bring to a rolling boil
again. Cook for additional 2 minutes at a rolling boil
that cannot be stirred down.

Cool 20 minutes. Pour into hot sterilized jars*
to within ½ inch of top, wipe rims clean and screw
on lids. When cool, press middle of lid. If it springs
back, lid is not sealed and jar should be refrigerated.
Store sealed jars in pantry. Makes about 3 pints
or 6 half-pints.

*Page 163: Instructions for sterilizing jars and lids.

Homemade Plum Jelly

6 - 6½ pounds ripe plums, peeled, pitted
1 (1.7 ounce) box fruit pectin
7 cups sugar

Cover plums with water and boil for 15 to 20 minutes.
Mash enough plums through strainer or sieve to equal
5 cups strained juice. Pour into saucepan with pectin
and bring to rolling boil.

Add sugar, bring back to a rolling boil and cook for
5 minutes, stirring constantly. Skim foam and pour
into hot sterilized jars* to within ½ inch of top, wipe
rims clean and screw on lids.

Place jars in water bath** to cover and heat in boiling
water for at least 10 minutes. Cool before tightening
lids completely. Makes about 8 to 10 pints.

*Page 163: Instructions for sterilizing jars and lids.
**Page 163-165: Instructions for water bath.

*Wild plum trees used to have thorns,
but the thorns were bred out over
thousands of years of cultivation.*

Dried Apricot Jam

1½ pints dried apricots
3¾ cups apple juice
2 lemons, juiced
3 cups sugar
¼ cup blanched, chopped almonds

Soak apricots overnight in apple juice. Pour mixture into saucepan; add lemon juice and grated lemon peels (grate yellow part only). Bring to a boil and simmer for about 20 minutes.

Add sugar, bring to a boil, stirring constantly, until sugar dissolves, about 20 minutes. Remove from heat and stir in almonds. Let stand for about 10 minutes. Pour into hot sterilized jars* to within ½ inch of top, wipe rims clean and screw on lids.

Place jars in water bath** to cover and heat in boiling water for at least 10 minutes. Cool before tightening lids completely.   Makes about 5 pints.

*Page 163: Instructions for sterilizing jars and lids.
**Page 163-165: Instructions for water bath.

Fig Jam

1¼ - 1¾ pounds figs, seeded
1 (6 ounce) box lemon gelatin
3 cups sugar

Crush enough figs to equal 3 cups. Bring all ingredients to a boil in saucepan, reduce heat and simmer for 10 minutes or until mixture thickens.

Pour into hot sterilized jars* to within ½ inch of top, wipe rims clean and screw on lids.

Place jars in water bath** to cover and heat in boiling water for at least 10 minutes. Cool before tightening lids completely. Makes about 3 pints.

*Page 163: Instructions for sterilizing jars and lids.
**Page 163-165: Instructions for water bath.

A perfect summer day is when the sun is shining, the breeze is blowing, the birds are singing and the lawn mower is broken.

—James Dent

Rhubarb Jam

5 - 7 medium-large stalks rhubarb
3 cups sugar
1 (6 ounce) package strawberry gelatin

● Finely chop enough rhubarb to equal 4 cups. Combine
with sugar and ½ cup water in large saucepan and
gently boil until tender; stir frequently. Remove from
heat, add gelatin and stir well.

● Pour into hot sterilized jars* to within ½ inch of top,
wipe rims clean and screw on lids.

● Place jars in water bath** to cover and heat in boiling
water for at least 10 minutes. Cool before tightening
lids completely. Makes about 4 pints.

*Page 163: Instructions for sterilizing jars and lids.
**Page 163-165: Instructions for water bath.

*If your jam is too thick, it may be
the result of cooking too long at a
temperature that is too low or it may be
an indication of not enough stirring.*

Special
Strawberry-Fig Jam

1 - 1½ pounds figs, stems trimmed
3 cups sugar
2 (6 ounce) packages strawberry gelatin
4 drops red food coloring

Finely chop enough figs to equal 3 cups. Pour into saucepan, add sugar and cook until figs are tender. Add gelatin and stir until it dissolves.

Pour into hot sterilized jars* to within ½ inch of top, wipe rims clean and screw on lids.

Place jars in water bath** to cover and heat in boiling water for at least 10 minutes. Cool before tightening lids completely. Makes about 4 pints.

*Page 163: Instructions for sterilizing jars and lids.
**Page 163-165: Instructions for water bath.

Easy Ice Box Strawberry Jam

1 (1 pint) carton strawberries, sliced
¼ cup honey
¼ teaspoon finely grated lemon peel

🍓 Place all ingredients in saucepan and bring to a boil. Simmer over medium-low heat, stirring occasionally for about 40 minutes until mixture thickens.

🍓 Pour into clean jars to within ½ inch of top, screw on lid and refrigerate. Makes about 2 cups or 1 pint.

The son of a farmer joined the army. On his first trip home after basic training, his father asked him, "How's army life?" His son replied, "Real good. The food is good, the work is easy and they let you sleep real late in the morning."

Kickin' Apricot Preserves

5 pounds apricots, pitted
Juice of 1 lemon
1 (1.7 ounce) box fruit pectin
1 tablespoon butter
6 cups sugar
3 ounces amaretto liqueur

● Slice apricots into ½-inch pieces and cook in saucepan with 2 cups water until tender. Add lemon juice, pectin and butter, bring to a boil and remove from heat.

● Add sugar and bring back to a boil for 1 minute, stirring constantly. Remove from heat and add amaretto. Pour into hot sterilized jars* to within ½ inch of top, wipe rims clean and screw on lids.

● Place jars in water bath** to cover and heat in boiling water for at least 10 minutes. Cool before tightening lids completely. Makes about 5 to 6 pints.

*Page 163: Instructions for sterilizing jars and lids.
**Page 163-165: Instructions for water bath.

Peach Preserves

1 - 1½ pounds (underripe) peaches
1½ - 2 cups sugar

Peel and chop enough peaches to equal 3 cups. Cook with ¼ cup water in large saucepan over medium heat, stirring frequently, for about 5 minutes or until barely tender.

Drain juice into measuring cup and pour into second saucepan. Add 2 cups sugar for 1 cup juice. Boil juice, stirring constantly, until sugar spins a thread.

Add peaches and cook at rapid boil for 4 to 5 minutes. Remove from heat; skim if necessary. Pour into hot sterilized jars* to within ½ inch of top, wipe rims clean and screw on lids.

Place jars in water bath** to cover and heat in boiling water for at least 10 minutes. Cool before tightening lids completely. Makes about 1 pint.

*Page 163: Instructions for sterilizing jars and lids.
**Page 163-165: Instructions for water bath.

Pear Preserves

10 pounds pears, peeled, sliced
2 pounds sugar

Place pears in large bowl, spread sugar over top, cover
and let stand overnight.

Pour pears and juice into large saucepan, add enough
water to cover by 1 to 2 inches, and bring mixture to
a boil. Reduce heat to simmer and cook until syrup
thickens, probably several hours.

Pour into hot sterilized jars* to within ½ inch of top,
wipe rims clean and screw on lids.

Place jars in water bath** to cover and heat in boiling
water for at least 10 minutes. Cool before tightening
lids completely. Makes about 10 pints.

*Page 163: Instructions for sterilizing jars and lids.
**Page 163-165: Instructions for water bath.

*I feel a recipe is only a theme, which
an intelligent cook can play each time with
a variation.*
                                        —Madame Benoit

Easy Strawberry Preserves

2 (1 quart) cartons strawberries, stemmed
7 cups sugar
1 teaspoon Epsom salt

🍓 Finely chop enough strawberries to equal 4 cups
and pour into large saucepan. Add sugar and Epsom
salt, stir frequently, cook over medium heat for about
10 minutes; stir frequently.

🍓 Skim foam off top. Pour into hot sterilized jars*
to within ½ inch of top, wipe rims clean and screw
on lids.

🍓 Place jars in water bath** to cover and heat in boiling
water for at least 10 minutes. Cool before tightening
lids completely. Makes about 4 pints.

*Page 163: Instructions for sterilizing jars and lids.
**Page 163-165: Instructions for water bath.

*Like apples and plums, strawberries are
a member of the rose family.*

Tomato Preserves

5 pounds ripe tomatoes
8 cups sugar
2 lemons, thinly sliced

Dip tomatoes in boiling water, peel and let stand overnight. Drain juice into saucepan, add sugar and boil rapidly until mixture spins a thread.

Add tomatoes and lemons and boil until thick and clear. Pour into hot sterilized jars* to within ½ inch of top, wipe rims clean and screw on lids.

Place jars in water bath** to cover and heat in boiling water for at least 10 minutes. Cool before tightening lids completely. Makes about 6 pints.

*Page 163: Instructions for sterilizing jars and lids.
**Page 163-165: Instructions for water bath.

What do you call a sleeping bull?

A bulldozer.

Orange Marmalade

4 - 5 oranges, peeled, sliced
3 - 4 lemons, peeled, sliced
Sugar

- Place fruit in large glass bowl and cover with 6 cups water. Let stand overnight. Pour mixture into saucepan and cook over medium-high heat about 30 minutes or until tender. Let stand overnight.

- On third day, add 2 cups sugar for each 1 pint of fruit. Cook fruit and sugar over medium heat until it reaches jelly consistency, about 10 minutes.

- Pour into hot sterilized jars* to within ½ inch of top, wipe rims clean and screw on lids.

- Place jars in water bath** to cover and heat in boiling water for at least 10 minutes. Cool before tightening lids completely. Makes about 7 pints.

*Page 163: Instructions for sterilizing jars and lids.
**Page 163-165: Instructions for water bath.

Where do apples like to go on vacation?

Fuji.

Brandied Cranberry-Orange Marmalade

2 cups fresh cranberries
1 cup brandy
⅔ cup orange juice
2 tablespoons grated orange peel

- Place cranberries in quart jar and pour brandy over top. Let stand for 48 hours and drain.

- Pour cranberries, orange juice and orange peel in large pot and bring to a boil. Reduce heat to low, stir occasionally, and cook about 15 minutes or until cranberries pop.

- Pour into hot sterilized jars* to within ½ inch of top, wipe rims clean and screw on lids.

- Place jars in water bath** to cover and heat in boiling water for at least 10 minutes. Cool before tightening lids completely. Makes about 1 pint.

*Page 163: Instructions for sterilizing jars and lids.
**Page 163-165: Instructions for water bath.

Sassy Apple Butter

2½ - 3 pounds apples, peeled, cored, chopped
5 cups sugar
½ cup vinegar
1 (8 ounce) box Red Hots® cinnamon candy

🍎 Process enough apples to equal 8 cups chopped
   and place in large saucepan. Add remaining
   ingredients, stir well and cook on medium-high for
   about 30 minutes; stir frequently.

🍎 Pour into hot sterilized jars* to within ½ inch of top,
   wipe rims clean and screw on lids.

🍎 Place jars in water bath** to cover and heat in boiling
   water for at least 10 minutes. Cool before tightening
   lids completely. Makes 6 pints.

*Page 163: Instructions for sterilizing jars and lids.
**Page 163-165: Instructions for water bath.

*Gardening requires a lot of water… most
of it in the form of perspiration.*

—Lou Erickson

Apricot Butter

4 pounds apricots, pitted, quartered
Honey

Place apricots in large saucepan with ¼ cup water and cook over medium heat. Stir frequently and mash apricots as they soften. Continue mashing while cooking.

Strain to remove peels. Return to heat and cook until it thickens. Sweeten with honey to taste. Pour into hot sterilized jars* to within ½ inch of top, wipe rims clean and screw on lids.

Place jars in water bath** to cover and heat in boiling water for at least 10 minutes. Cool before tightening lids completely. Makes about 8 pints.

*Page 163: Instructions for sterilizing jars and lids.
**Page 163-165: Instructions for water bath.

After all is said and done, a lot more is said than done.
—Murphy's Law

Grape Butter

1 gallon (8 - 9 pounds) grapes
Honey

🍇 Place grapes in large saucepan or soup pot with ¼ cup
water and cook over medium heat. Stir frequently
and mash as grapes soften.

🍇 Strain to remove skin and seeds. Return to heat and
cook until thick. Add honey to sweeten. Pour into
hot sterilized jars* to within ½ inch of top, wipe rims
clean and screw on lids.

🍇 Place jars in water bath** to cover and heat in boiling
water for at least 10 minutes. Cool before tightening
lids completely. Makes about 9 pints.

*Page 163: Instructions for sterilizing jars and lids.
**Page 163-165: Instructions for water bath.

*A magical tractor was driving down the
road and turned into a field.*

Peach Butter

4 pounds peaches, pitted

🍅 Peel or parboil peaches to remove skin. Place in large saucepan with one-third amount of water to peaches. Simmer to soften peaches; stir frequently. Puree in food processor or blender.

🍅 Pour into baking pan and bake, uncovered, at 325° for 1 hour. Remove from oven, stir well and continue to bake, stirring every 15 to 20 minutes, until mixture is thick and reddish amber color.

🍅 Pour into hot sterilized jars* to within ½ inch of top, wipe rims clean and screw on lids.

🍅 Place jars in water bath** to cover and heat in boiling water for at least 10 minutes. Cool before tightening lids completely. Makes about 8 to 10 pints.

*Page 163: Instructions for sterilizing jars and lids.
**Page 163-165: Instructions for water bath.

Pear Honey

4 - 5 pounds ripe pears, peeled, cored
1 (8 ounce) can crushed pineapple
1 lemon, juiced
5 cups sugar

Process enough pears to equal 9 cups puree and add
to saucepan. Stir in pineapple, lemon juice and sugar.
Grate only yellow peel of lemon and add to mixture.
Cook on low for about 20 minutes.

Pour into hot sterilized jars* to within ½ inch of top,
wipe rims clean and screw on lids.

Place jars in water bath** to cover and heat in boiling
water for at least 10 minutes. Cool before tightening
lids completely. Makes about 6 pints.

*Page 163: Instructions for sterilizing jars and lids.
**Page 163-165: Instructions for water bath.

*A man should never plant a garden
larger than his wife can take care of.*
—T.H. Everett

Apple Pie Apples

4 - 5 pounds apples, peeled, sliced
5 cups sugar
6 tablespoons tapioca

● Prepare enough apples to equal 12 cups sliced. Mix all ingredients with 3 cups water.

● Pour into hot sterilized jars* to within ½ inch of top, wipe rims clean and screw on lids.

● Place jars in water bath** to cover and heat in boiling water for at least 10 minutes. Cool before tightening lids completely.   Makes enough for 4 pies.

*Page 163: Instructions for sterilizing jars and lids.
**Page 163-165: Instructions for water bath.

Hot water canning uses a canner or large pot with flat bottom and rack to hold jars. It is the best way to seal sterilized jars to prevent bacteria growth in food.

Spiced Figs

6½ - 7 pounds firm, ripe figs
5 cups sugar, divided
3 cups vinegar
1 teaspoon whole cloves
1 tablespoon whole allspice berries
2 sticks cinnamon

● Peel or parboil figs to remove skins and pits; set aside
   to cool and drain. Add 3 cups sugar and 1½ quarts
   water to separate saucepan and cook on medium heat
   until sugar dissolves; stir occasionally. Add figs and
   simmer for 30 minutes.

● Add remaining sugar and vinegar. Tie spices in
   cloth bag and add to figs. Cook gently until figs are
   translucent. Cover and let stand for 12 to 24 hours in
   cool place. Remove spice bag; heat to simmer.

● Pour into hot sterilized jars* to within ½ inch of top,
   wipe rims clean and screw on lids.

● Place jars in water bath** to cover and heat in boiling
   water for at least 10 minutes. Cool before tightening
   lids completely. Makes about 8 pints.

*Page 163: Instructions for sterilizing jars and lids.
**Page 163-165: Instructions for water bath.

Brandied Peaches

9 cups sugar
2 cinnamon sticks
1 tablespoon whole cloves
5 pounds peaches, peeled, pitted, halved
1⅔ cups brandy

● Dissolve sugar in 2½ cups water. Place cinnamon and cloves in cheesecloth bag and add to water. Bring to a boil; add peaches a few at a time and cook until peaches are just tender.

● Place colander over bowl, drain peaches and save syrup. Bring syrup to a boil until it thickens slightly. Add brandy and stir.

● Pack peaches into sterilized jars* to within ½ inch of top. Pour syrup over top, wipe rims clean and screw on lids.

● Place jars in water bath** to cover and heat in boiling water for at least 10 minutes. Cool before tightening lids completely. Makes about 8 to 9 pints.

*Page 163: Instructions for sterilizing jars and lids.
**Page 163-165: Instructions for water bath.

Pickled Peaches

5 cups sugar
1¼ cups vinegar
¼ cup whole cloves
5 pounds small white clingstone peaches, peeled
8 (2 - 3 inch) cinnamon sticks
1 tablespoon nutmeg, optional

Boil sugar, vinegar and 1¼ cups water in large pot
for about 5 to 7 minutes to make syrup. Stick cloves
into peaches and add to pot. Add cinnamon sticks and
nutmeg wrapped in cheesecloth bag. Return syrup to
boil and cook for about 25 minutes or until peaches
are tender.

Remove cinnamon sticks and nutmeg bag. Pour
peaches and syrup into sterilized jars* to within
1 inch of top, wipe rims clean and screw on lids.

Place jars in water bath** to cover and heat in boiling
water for at least 10 minutes. Cool before tightening
lids completely. Makes about 9 to 10 pints.

*Page 163: Instructions for sterilizing jars and lids.
**Page 163-165: Instructions for water bath.

Pickled Pears

3 pounds pears, peeled, sliced or chopped
Juice of 2 lemons
1½ pounds sugar
4 cups cider vinegar
3 cinnamon sticks
3 star anise
1 teaspoon whole cloves
1 teaspoon peppercorns
1 teaspoon allspice

Toss pears with lemon juice. Place in large saucepan with remaining ingredients and bring to a boil. Reduce heat and cook until pears are tender.

Spoon into sterilized* jars and pour syrup over top to within ½ inch of top, wipe rims clean and screw on lids.

Place jars in water bath** to cover and heat in boiling water for at least 10 minutes. Cool before tightening lids completely. Makes about 3 to 4 quarts.

*Page 163: Instructions for sterilizing jars and lids.
**Page 163-165: Instructions for water bath.

*Like a prune, we're not getting any
better looking, but we are getting sweeter.*
—N.D. Stice

Easy Plum Sauce

This is great with chicken, turkey or pork.

4 pounds plums, peeled, pitted
¾ cup minced white onion
2 tablespoons canned diced green chilies
1 clove garlic
1 (1 inch) piece fresh ginger
2 tablespoons mustard seed
1 cup cider vinegar
1 cup white vinegar
2 cups packed brown sugar

- Puree plums, onions, green chilies, garlic, ginger and mustard seed in food processor or blender. Combine vinegars and brown sugar in large saucepan, bring to a gentle boil and reduce heat; stir frequently.

- Pour plum mixture into saucepan and cook for about 1 hour 30 minutes or until thick and syrupy.

- Pour into hot sterilized jars* to within ½ inch of top, wipe rims clean and screw on lids.

- Place jars in water bath** to cover and heat in boiling water for at least 10 minutes. Cool before tightening lids completely. Makes about 4 pints.

*Page 163: Instructions for sterilizing jars and lids.
**Page 163-165: Instructions for water bath.

Aunt Eva's Watermelon Rind Pickles

About 7 pounds watermelon rind
1 cup lime juice
1 quart vinegar
5 pounds sugar
6 - 7 cinnamon sticks
1 teaspoon whole cloves
1 teaspoon mace

Remove all green outer edges and all red inner edges of watermelon rind. Cut into 3-inch pieces and place in large ceramic crock or glass container.

Mix lime juice with enough water to cover rind, pour into container and soak rind overnight.

Pour off liquid, rinse rind in cold water and drain. Mix vinegar, sugar and spices and pour vinegar mixture over rind in crock. Add enough water to cover rind and soak overnight.

Continued next page...

Continued from previous page...

- On third day, cook rind mixture for 20 minutes over low heat. Pour into hot sterilized jars* to within ½ inch of top, wipe rims clean and screw on lids.

- Place jars in water bath** to cover and heat in boiling water for at least 10 minutes. Cool before tightening lids completely. Makes about 6 pints

TIP: If you want to brighten the rinds, add food coloring.

*Page 163: Instructions for sterilizing jars and lids.
**Page 163-165: Instructions for water bath.

I do not like broccoli. And I haven't liked it since I was a little kid and my mother made me eat it. Now I'm the President of the United States of America and I'm not going to eat broccoli any more.

—President George H.W. Bush, 1990

Pickled Vegetables, Relishes & Chow-Chows

Contents

Pickled Asparagus Spears

1 pound fresh asparagus spears, trimmed
Garlic cloves
Dill weed
Cayenne pepper
2½ cups vinegar
¼ cup pickling salt

● Pack asparagus into sterilized* jars to within 1 inch
  of top. Add to each jar garlic, dill weed and cayenne
  pepper to taste.

● Bring vinegar, pickling salt and 2½ cups water to
  boil, pour over asparagus, wipe rims clean and screw
  on lids.

● Place jars in water bath** to cover and heat in boiling
  water for at least 10 minutes. Cool before tightening
  lids completely. Makes about 1 to 2 pints.

*Page 163: Instructions for sterilizing jars and lids.
**Page 163-165: Instructions for water bath.

*Jars that are not sealed properly must
be refrigerated. (See page 165.)*

Pickled Beets

15 pounds beetroot, peeled, trimmed
4 cups sugar
2 cups vinegar
1 teaspoon pickling spice

● Place enough beets in 5 sterilized* quart jars to within 1 inch of top.

● Combine 2 cups water with remaining ingredients in large saucepan and bring to rolling boil. Pour over beets. Wipe rims clean and screw on lids.

● Place jars in water bath** to cover and heat in boiling water for at least 10 minutes. Cool before tightening lids completely. Makes about 5 quarts.

*Page 163: Instructions for sterilizing jars and lids.
**Page 163-165: Instructions for water bath.

There are two types of canning: water bath canning and pressure-cooker canning. Water bath is the easiest and is featured exclusively in this cookbook.

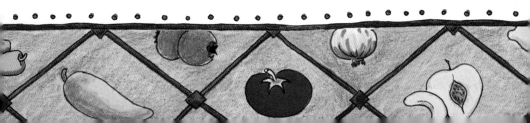

Easy Sauerkraut

1 - 2 heads cabbage, shredded
2 teaspoons vinegar
1 teaspoon sugar
1 teaspoon pickling salt

Place shredded cabbage loosely to within 1 inch of top
of sterilized* quart jar. Combine vinegar, sugar and
pickling salt with 1 quart water in saucepan; bring
to a boil.

Pour hot liquid over cabbage and wipe rim clean.
Tighten sterilized lid and ring on jar. Place in cold
water bath for 30 minutes.

When cool, press middle of lid. If it springs back, lid
is not sealed and jar must be refrigerated. Store
sealed jar in pantry for 6 weeks before serving.
Makes about 1 quart.

*Page 163: Instructions for sterilizing jars and lids.

Sauerkraut is a German word meaning
"sour cabbage". But the first known
instances of sauerkraut were in China
more than 1,000 years before the dish
appeared in Europe.

Easy Winter Sweet Corn

This is an old Amish recipe used for years.

Corn-on-the-cob, shucked, silked*
Pickling salt
Sugar

🍅 Cut corn off cobs into large bowl. Add a little pickling salt and a little sugar to taste and stir well.

🍅 Pour into hot sterilized jars** to within ½ inch of top, wipe rims clean and screw on lids.

🍅 Place jars in cold water in canner or flat-bottomed soup pot with towel padding inside. Cook on medium for about 3 hours. Store sealed jars in pantry.

*TIP: 1½ to 2 ears corn will equal about 1 cup kernels. 2 cups will fit into 1 pint jar.

**Page 163: Instructions for sterilizing jars and lids.

New gardeners learn by trowel and error.

Dill Pickles

Whole cucumbers
Vinegar
Fresh dill with seeds
2 ($\frac{1}{2}$ quart) bottles distilled water
1 (32 ounce) bottle vinegar
1 cup pickling salt

- Cook cucumbers over medium heat in enough vinegar to cover until cucumbers turn pale green. Drain cucumbers and set vinegar aside for next batch.

- Pack cucumbers into sterilized quart or pint jars* to within 1 inch of top. Stuff 4 to 5 big stems fresh dill and 2 teaspoons dill seed into each quart jar. (Use half this amount for pint jars.)

- Mix distilled water, vinegar and salt, bring to a boil and pour over cucumbers to within ½ inch of top, wipe rims clean and screw on lids.

- Place jars in water bath** to cover and heat in boiling water for at least 10 minutes for pints and 15 minutes for quarts. Cool before tightening lids completely.

*Page 163: Instructions for sterilizing jars and lids.
**Page 163-165: Instructions for water bath.

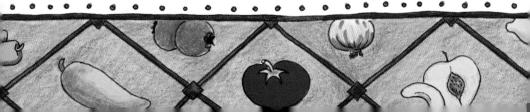

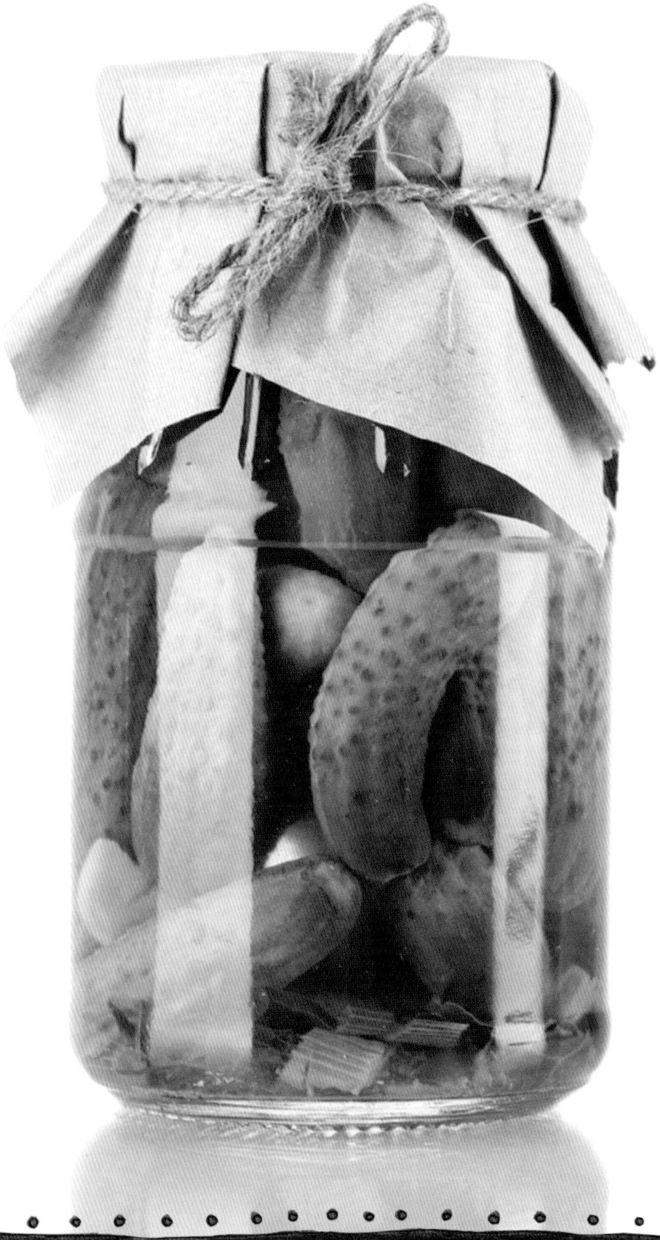

Dandy Dills

10 pounds pickling cucumbers
5 medium onions, chopped
32 cloves garlic
32 small hot peppers
16 bay leaves
Fresh dill
Mustard seed
32 whole allspice berries
32 whole cloves
32 peppercorns
4 cups vinegar
1½ cups pickling salt

● Pack about 14 to 16 sterilized* pint jars with
  cucumbers, onions, 2 cloves garlic, 2 hot peppers,
  1 bay leaf, dill, mustard seeds and 2 each of
  remaining seasonings.

● Bring 4 quarts water, vinegar and pickling salt to
  a boil in heavy saucepan. Pour into jars to within
  ½ inch of top, wipe rims clean and screw on lids.

● Place jars in water bath** to cover and heat in boiling
  water for at least 10 minutes. Cool before tightening
  lids completely. Makes about 16 pints.

*Page 163: Instructions for sterilizing jars and lids.
**Page 163-165: Instructions for water bath.

Gus's Garlic Pickles

10 - 15 pounds pickling cucumbers
Small hot peppers
Garlic cloves, peeled
1 cup vinegar
⅓ cup pickling salt
Fresh dill sprigs

- Pack cucumbers in sterilized* jars with 1 pepper and 1 garlic clove in each jar.

- Bring 2 cups water, vinegar and pickling salt to a boil and fill sterilized jars* to within ½ inch of top.

- Place 1 or 2 dill sprigs on top of each jar, wipe rims clean and screw on lids.

- Place jars in water bath** to cover and heat in boiling water for at least 10 minutes. Cool before tightening lids completely. Pickles will be ready in about 3 weeks.

*Page 163: Instructions for sterilizing jars and lids.
**Page 163-165: Instructions for water bath.

No one is good at everything but everyone is good at something.

Granny's Cucumber Spears

7 pounds seedless cucumbers, peeled
2 cups pickling lime
1 (2 ounce) box powdered ginger

- Slice cucumbers lengthwise into spears.

- Dissolve lime in 2 gallons water, add spears and soak for 24 hours. Drain and thoroughly rinse 3 times.

- Mix ginger with 2 gallons water, soak cucumbers in mixture for 6 hours and drain; do not rinse.

Brine:

5 pounds sugar
2 quarts vinegar
1 teaspoon celery seed
1 teaspoon allspice
1 teaspoon cloves

- Mix sugar and vinegar in large saucepan, stir to dissolve sugar and add spices. Add cucumbers and let stand for 1 hour. Bring to a boil, reduce heat and cook slowly for 1 hour.

- Pack cucumbers into sterilized jars* to within ½ inch of top, pour brine over top, within ½ inch of top, wipe rims clean and screw on lids.

Continued next page...

Continued from previous page...

 Place jars in water bath** to cover and heat in boiling water for at least 10 minutes. Cool before tightening lids completely. Makes about 7 quarts.

*Page 163: Instructions for sterilizing jars and lids.
**Page 163-165: Instructions for water bath.

Peter Piper picked a peck of pickled peppers,

A peck of pickled peppers Peter Piper picked.

If Peter Piper picked a peck of pickled peppers,

Where's the peck of pickled peppers Peter Piper picked?

—Mother Goose

Annie B's
Bread-and-Butter Pickles

*My grandmother gave me this family recipe. It is
more than 100 years old and still used today.*

25 large cucumbers
12 onions
½ cup pickling salt
2 cups vinegar
2 cups sugar
2 tablespoons mustard seed
2 tablespoons turmeric
2 tablespoons ginger

Soak cucumbers overnight in water. Slice cucumbers
and onions, add pickling salt and let stand for 1 hour;
rinse well.

Mix vinegar, sugar, mustard seed, turmeric and
ginger. Bring to a boil, add cucumbers and onions and
boil for 40 minutes.

Pour into hot sterilized jars* to within ½ inch of top,
wipe rims clean and screw on lids.

Continued next page...

Continued from previous page...

Place jars in water bath** to cover and heat in boiling water for at least 10 minutes. Cool before tightening lids completely. Makes about 10 to 12 pints.

*Page 163: Instructions for sterilizing jars and lids.
**Page 163-165: Instructions for water bath.

The best way to garden is to put on a wide-brimmed straw hat and some old clothes. Get a hoe in one hand and a cold drink in the other and tell someone else where to dig.

—Texas Bix Bender
Don't Throw in the Trowel

Quick
Bread-and-Butter Pickles

1 quart jar whole dill pickles
1½ cups sugar
1 onion, sliced
2 cinnamon sticks
2 tablespoons vinegar

Drain pickles and slice into large bowl; add all
ingredients and mix well. Return to washed original
jar and tighten lid.

Let stand at room temperature for 4 to 5 days and
turn jar upside down every other day. Store in
refrigerator. Makes 1 quart.

*Farmers are real experts. They are
often outstanding in their fields.*

Sweet Hot Pickles

1 (1 gallon) jar or 4 (1 quart) jars whole dill pickles,
   drained, rinsed
4 pounds sugar
6 cloves garlic, chopped
1 (5 ounce) bottle hot sauce

- Place rinsed and drained pickles in large pot. Add sugar, garlic and hot sauce and stir well.

- Pour into original 1-gallon jar or 4 (1 quart) jars and let stand for 6 days in refrigerator. Turn jar upside down every day.

- After 6 days, the pickles are ready to serve. Store in refrigerator. Makes 1 gallon or 4 quarts.

Pack vegetables and fruits tightly in hot jars and pour hot or boiling syrup or liquid to within ½ inch of top. This allows for food to expand and for a proper seal to occur.

Cucumber-Tomato Medley

Cucumbers, peeled
Tomatoes
Pickling salt

● Trim ends of cucumbers and slice. Scald tomatoes
in boiling water and remove skin. Quarter or
chop tomatoes and pack into sterilized* jars with
cucumbers to within 1 inch of top.

● To each pint jar, add ½ teaspoon pickling salt; or add
1 teaspoon pickling salt to each quart jar. Wipe rims
clean and screw on lids.

● Place jars in water bath** to cover and heat in boiling
water for 35 minutes for pint jars and 45 minutes for
quart jars; cool before tightening lids completely.

*Page 163: Instructions for sterilizing jars and lids.
**Page 163-165: Instructions for water bath.

*There's some truth to the old saying,
"cool as a cucumber". The interior of a
cucumber can be as much as 20 degrees
cooler than the temperature outside.*

Pickled Green Beans

4 heads dill or 2 - 3 tablespoons dill seeds
4 cloves garlic, peeled
2 pounds fresh tender green beans
¼ cup pickling salt
2 cups vinegar

Place dill head or seeds and garlic clove in each of 4 sterilized* pint jars. Snap ends of beans off and place in sterilized jars.

Combine salt, vinegar and 2 cups water in saucepan and bring to a boil.

Pour liquid into jars to within ½ inch of top, wipe rims clean and screw on lids.

Place jars in water bath** to cover and heat in boiling water for at least 10 minutes. Cool before tightening lids completely. Makes about 4 pints.

*Page 163: Instructions for sterilizing jars and lids.
**Page 163-165: Instructions for water bath.

What do you call two recently married spiders?

Newly webs.

Pickled Jalapeno Slices

Jalapenos, stemmed, seeded, sliced
Distilled vinegar
Olive oil
Pickling salt

● Stuff jalapenos, 1 tablespoon distilled vinegar,
½ teaspoon olive oil and ½ teaspoon pickling salt into
each hot sterilized* pint jar. Pour boiling water over
jalapenos to within ½ inch of top, wipe rims clean and
screw on lids.

● Place jars in cold water bath for 35 minutes. When
cool, press middle of lid. If it springs back, lid is not
sealed and jar should be refrigerated. Store sealed jars
in pantry.

*Page 163: Instructions for sterilizing jars and lids.

*My wife's a water sign. I'm an earth sign.
Together we make mud.*

—Rodney Dangerfield

Party Pickled Okra

Small okra pods with stems, trimmed
Garlic cloves
Jalapenos
Vinegar

● Place okra, 2 cloves garlic and 1 jalapeno in each
   sterilized* pint jar.

● Bring equal amounts of water and vinegar to boil
   and pour into hot sterilized jars to within ½ inch of
   top, wipe rims clean and screw on lids.

● Place jars in water bath** to cover and heat in
   boiling water for at least 10 minutes. Cool before
   tightening lids completely. Store sealed jars in
   pantry for 3 weeks before serving.

*Page 163: Instructions for sterilizing jars and lids.
**Page 163-165: Instructions for water bath.

Life is not a dress rehearsal.

Okra-Tomato Mix-Up

Okra
Tomatoes
Pickling salt

Trim ends off okra and slice; scald tomatoes in boiling water to remove peel, then quarter or leave whole.

Pack into hot sterilized jars* to within ½ inch of top, add ½ teaspoon pickling salt for 1 pint and 1 teaspoon pickling salt for 1 quart jar, wipe rims clean and screw on lids.

Place jars in water bath** to cover and heat in boiling water for at least 35 minutes for pint jars and 45 minutes for quart jars (Add water if necessary. Bring back to rapid boil and reset timer to entire processing time.) Cool before tightening lids completely.

*Page 163: Instructions for sterilizing jars and lids.
**Page 163-165: Instructions for water bath.

My mother's menu consisted of two things: take it or leave it.

—Buddy Hackett

Peter Piper's Pickled Peppers

2 teaspoons mustard seed, divided
2 teaspoons whole allspice, divided
2 teaspoons pickling salt, divided
2½ cups vinegar
½ cup sugar
6 green bell peppers, cored, seeded, quartered
6 red bell peppers, cored, seeded, quartered

Place ½ teaspoon mustard seed, ½ teaspoon whole allspice and ½ teaspoon pickling salt in each of 4 sterilized pint jars*.

Bring vinegar, sugar and 2½ cups water to a boil in large saucepan; add peppers and heat thoroughly.

Pour into hot sterilized jars to within ½ inch of top, wipe rims clean and screw on lids.

Place jars in water bath** to cover and heat in boiling water for at least 10 minutes. Cool before tightening lids completely. Makes about 4 pints.

*Page 163: Instructions for sterilizing jars and lids.
**Page 163-165: Instructions for water bath.

Pickled Summer Squash

4 pounds summer squash
3 large onions
1 cup vinegar
1¾ cups sugar
½ cup chopped green bell pepper
½ teaspoon mustard seed
½ teaspoon celery seed

🍅 Prepare enough sliced or whole squash to equal 8 cups and enough sliced onions to equal 2 cups.

🍅 Add all ingredients, except squash, to large saucepan and bring to a rolling boil. Add squash and boil for 1 minute.

🍅 Pour into hot sterilized jars* to within ½ inch of top, wipe rims clean and screw on lids.

🍅 Place jars in water bath** to cover and heat in boiling water for at least 10 minutes. Cool before tightening lids completely. Makes about 7 pints.

*Page 163: Instructions for sterilizing jars and lids.
**Page 163-165: Instructions for water bath.

Easy Cold-Packed
Tomatoes

Fresh tomatoes

- Peel or blanch tomatoes to remove skins. Pack whole or quartered tomatoes into hot sterilized jars* to within ½ inch of top, wipe rims clean and screw on lids.

- Place jars in water bath** to cover and heat in boiling water for 35 minutes for pint jars and 45 minutes for quart jars. Cool before tightening lids completely.

TIP: *1 medium tomato equals about 1 cup chopped. 2 cups equal 1 pint.*

TIP: *After opening, store jars in refrigerator.*

*Page 163: Instructions for sterilizing jars and lids.
**Page 163-165: Instructions for water bath.

How do you fix a broken tomato?

Tomato paste

Easy Hot-Packed Tomatoes

Fresh ripe tomatoes

Peel or blanch tomatoes to remove skins. Cut in wedges or leave whole and place in large saucepan. Gently boil tomatoes for 5 minutes with just enough water to cover.

Place tomatoes into hot sterilized jars* and pour liquid to within ½ inch of top, wipe rims clean and screw on lids.

Place jars in water bath** to cover and heat in boiling water for at least 10 minutes for pint jars and 15 minutes for quart jars. Cool before tightening lids completely.

*Page 163: Instructions for sterilizing jars and lids.
**Page 163-165: Instructions for water bath.

What vegetable did Noah leave off the Ark?

Leeks.

Zucchini Toss-Up

4 - 4½ pounds zucchini, minced
8 - 10 medium carrots, diced
2 - 3 large white onions, minced
1 - 2 large bell peppers, cored, seeded, diced
2¼ cups white vinegar
¼ cup sugar
2 tablespoons pickling salt
1 tablespoon celery seed
¾ teaspoon dry mustard

🍅 Mince enough zucchini to equal 4 cups, enough diced carrots to equal 3 cups, enough minced onion to equal 3 cups and enough diced bell peppers to equal 1½ cups.

🍅 Mix all ingredients in large skillet. Saute over medium heat for 15 minutes or until tender.

🍅 Pour into hot sterilized jars* to within ½ inch of top, wipe rims clean and screw on lids.

🍅 Place jars in water bath** to cover and heat in boiling water for at least 10 minutes. Cool before tightening lids completely. Makes about 8 pints.

*Page 163: Instructions for sterilizing jars and lids.
**Page 163-165: Instructions for water bath.

Apple Relish

5 medium onions, quartered or chopped
2 hot peppers, stemmed, seeded, halved or chopped
1 tablespoon pickling salt
14 large red apples with peels, cored, halved or chopped
1 quart vinegar
1 cup sugar
1 tablespoon pickling spice
1 tablespoon whole cloves
1 stick cinnamon

● Grate onions and peppers; add pickling salt and
1 cup boiling water. Let stand for 15 minutes in large
saucepan and drain. Grate apples (with peels) and
mix with onion mixture.

● Add vinegar, sugar and spices wrapped in cheesecloth
to saucepan and cook on medium-high for 10 to
15 minutes.

● Pour into hot sterilized jars* to within ½ inch of top,
wipe rims clean and screw on lids.

● Place jars in water bath** to cover and heat in boiling
water for at least 10 minutes. Cool before tightening
lids completely. Makes about 9 pints.

*Page 163: Instructions for sterilizing jars and lids.
**Page 163-165: Instructions for water bath.

No-Cook Carrot Relish

4 large carrots, chopped
9 red bell peppers, cored, seeded, sliced
9 yellow bell peppers, cored, seeded, sliced
2 heads cabbage, chopped
7 onions, sliced
½ cup pickling salt

🍅 Mix above ingredients and let stand for 2 hours.
Drain and rinse.

6 cups vinegar
4 cups sugar
2 tablespoons mustard seed
2 tablespoons celery seed

🍅 Mix vinegar, sugar and seasonings; stir until sugar
dissolves. Pack vegetables into sterilized jars* to
within ½ inch of top. Pour vinegar mixture over
vegetables, wipe rims clean and screw on lids.

🍅 Place jars in water bath** to cover and heat in boiling
water for at least 10 minutes. Cool before tightening
lids completely. Makes about 16 pints.

*Page 163: Instructions for sterilizing jars and lids.
**Page 163-165: Instructions for water bath.

Fresh Corn Relish

6 - 8 ears fresh corn
2 heads cabbage, shredded
4 - 5 large onions, chopped
2 - 3 pounds ripe tomatoes, peeled, chopped
1 - 2 pounds cucumbers, peeled, chopped
2 (16 ounce) bottles vinegar
2 cups sugar
1 tablespoon pickling salt
1 tablespoon celery seed
$\frac{1}{2}$ tablespoon turmeric

● Cut off enough corn kernels to equal 4 cups, shred enough cabbage to equal 4 cups, chop enough onion to equal 4 cups, chop enough tomatoes to equal 4 cups and chop enough cucumbers to equal 4 cups.

● Mix all ingredients in large saucepan and cook slowly for about 15 minutes. Pour into hot sterilized jars* to within ½ inch of top, wipe rims clean and screw on lids.

● Place jars in water bath** to cover and heat in boiling water for at least 10 minutes. Cool before tightening lids completely. Makes about 16 pints.

*Page 163: Instructions for sterilizing jars and lids.
**Page 163-165: Instructions for water bath.

Sweet Corn Relish

1 cup vinegar
½ cup sugar
1½ teaspoons mustard seed
½ teaspoon pickling salt
6 - 7 ears corn, shucked, silked
½ - 1 medium bell pepper, minced
½ small white onion, minced
1 (4 ounce) jar diced pimento
1 small rib celery, minced
1 clove garlic, minced

🍅 Combine vinegar, sugar, mustard seed and pickling
salt in large saucepan and boil for 2 minutes. Stir to
dissolve sugar.

🍅 Prepare enough corn kernels off cobs to equal 3½ cups,
enough minced bell pepper to equal ½ cup and enough
minced onion to equal ¼ cup.

🍅 Add all ingredients to vinegar-sugar mixture and boil
3 minutes. Cool and refrigerate in airtight containers.
Makes 3 pints.

*Jars that are not sealed properly must
be refrigerated. (See page 165.)*

Onion Relish

This is a gorgeous amber color and is delicious.

3 - 4 pounds large white onions, chopped, sliced or diced
2 cups vinegar
2 cups sugar
1 teaspoon pickling salt

🍅 Prepare enough onions to equal 8 cups. Pour just enough boiling water over onions to cover and let stand 5 minutes. Drain.

🍅 Pour vinegar, sugar and pickling salt in large saucepan, add onions and simmer for 25 minutes.

🍅 Pour into hot sterilized jars* to within ½ inch of top, wipe rims clean and screw on lids.

🍅 Place jars in water bath** to cover and heat in boiling water for at least 10 minutes. Cool before tightening lids completely. Makes about 6 pints.

*Page 163: Instructions for sterilizing jars and lids.
**Page 163-165: Instructions for water bath.

Sweet Pepper Relish

12 green bell peppers, cored, seeded, finely chopped
12 red bell peppers, cored, seeded, finely chopped
15 medium onions, finely chopped
4 cups vinegar
5 cups sugar
2 tablespoons pickling salt

● Place vegetables in large saucepan. Bring vinegar,
sugar and pickling salt to a boil and pour over
vegetables. Gently boil until peppers are tender
(about 25 minutes).

● Pour into hot sterilized jars* to within ½ inch of top,
wipe rims clean and screw on lids.

● Place jars in water bath** to cover and heat in boiling
water for at least 10 minutes. Cool before tightening
lids completely. Makes about 7 pints.

*Page 163: Instructions for sterilizing jars and lids.
**Page 163-165: Instructions for water bath.

Hot Pepper Relish

4 pounds green tomatoes, minced
4 large onions, minced
4 - 6 large jalapenos, seeded, minced
2 - 4 bell peppers, cored, seeded, minced
1 quart vinegar
2 cups sugar
1 cup prepared mustard

Prepare enough minced tomatoes to equal 4 cups,
enough minced onion to equal 4 cups, enough minced
jalapenos to equal 4 cups and enough minced bell
pepper to equal 2 cups.

Mix all ingredients in large saucepan and bring to a
boil. Reduce heat to medium and cook for 10 minutes.

Pour into hot sterilized jars* to within ½ inch of top,
wipe rims clean and screw on lids.

Place jars in water bath** to cover and heat in boiling
water for at least 10 minutes. Cool before tightening
lids completely. Makes about 7 pints.

*Page 163: Instructions for sterilizing jars and lids.
**Page 163-165: Instructions for water bath.

Dad's Favorite Jalapeno Relish

5 pounds jalapenos, cored, seeded, minced*
2 pounds onions, peeled, minced
4 - 5 pods garlic, separated into cloves, peeled, minced
½ cup sugar
1 (1 quart) bottle vinegar
¼ cup mustard seed
¼ cup pickling salt

🌶 Mix all ingredients in large saucepan; cook over medium heat for 1 hour.

🌶 Pour into hot sterilized jars* to within ½ inch of top, wipe rims clean and screw on lids.

🌶 Place jars in water bath** to cover and heat in boiling water for at least 10 minutes. Cool before tightening lids completely. Makes about 6 pints.

*TIP: Wear rubber gloves when handling jalapenos and other hot peppers.

*Page 163: Instructions for sterilizing jars and lids.
**Page 163-165: Instructions for water bath.

Squash Pickle Relish

1½ - 2 pounds yellow squash
Pickling salt
3 cups sugar
2 cups vinegar
2 teaspoons mustard seed
2 teaspoons celery seed
2 cups (about 3 whole) chopped red bell peppers
2 cups (about 3 whole) chopped green bell peppers
2 large onions, thinly sliced in rings

Slice enough squash to equal 3 cups and place in salted ice water; let stand for 1 hour and drain well.

Combine sugar, vinegar and seasonings in large saucepan and bring to a boil. Add squash and remaining vegetables; boil for 5 minutes.

Pour into hot sterilized jars* to within ½ inch of top, wipe rims clean and screw on lids.

Place jars in water bath** to cover and heat in boiling water for at least 10 minutes. Cool before tightening lids completely. Makes about 3 to 4 pints.

*Page 163: Instructions for sterilizing jars and lids.
**Page 163-165: Instructions for water bath.

Old-Fashioned Chow-Chow

Chow-chow is a uniquely American pickled relish. This recipe is more than 100 years old and is still one of the best.

7 - 8 pounds tomatoes, peeled, minced
6 jalapenos, seeded, minced*
12 bell peppers, seeded, minced
12 medium onions, minced
2 large heads cabbage, shredded
¾ cup pickling salt

Mix vegetables with pickling salt in large bowl and stir well. Set aside for 2 hours and drain well.

6½ cups sugar
2 quarts vinegar
2 teaspoons grated ginger
1 teaspoon ground mustard
1 teaspoon ground cloves
1 teaspoon ground cinnamon
1 teaspoon turmeric
1 teaspoon celery seed

Mix sugar, vinegar and seasonings, except celery seed, in saucepan and gently boil for 20 minutes. Add celery seed, stir well and pour over vegetables.

Continued next page...

Continued from previous page...

Pour into hot sterilized jars* to within ½ inch of top, wipe rims clean and screw on lids.

Place jars in water bath** to cover and heat in boiling water for at least 10 minutes. Cool before tightening lids completely. Makes about 14 pints.

TIP: *Wear rubber gloves when handling hot peppers.*

*Page 163: Instructions for sterilizing jars and lids.
**Page 163-165: Instructions for water bath.

Grandma's Secret: Label top of lid with date and contents so you will not use the flat lid again. It is all right to reuse the screw-on ring that tightens the lid.

Happy Chow-Chow

1 - 2 heads cabbage, shredded
2 - 2½ pounds tomatoes, minced
4 large onions, grated
4 bell peppers, cored, seeded, minced
2 - 4 jalapenos, seeded, minced
1 (16 ounce) bottle vinegar
4 cups sugar
2 tablespoons mustard seed
2 tablespoons celery seed
2 tablespoons turmeric

Prepare enough shredded cabbage to equal 4 cups, enough minced tomatoes to equal 4 cups, enough grated onions to equal 4 cups, enough minced bell pepper to equal 4 cups. and enough minced jalapenos to equal 1 cup.

Combine all ingredients in large saucepan, bring to a boil (may take 45 minutes), reduce heat and cook on low about 10 minutes.

Pour into hot sterilized jars* to within ½ inch of top, wipe rims clean and screw on lids.

Place jars in water bath** to cover and heat in boiling water for at least 10 minutes. Cool before tightening lids completely. Makes about 14 pints.

*Page 163: Instructions for sterilizing jars and lids.
**Page 163-165: Instructions for water bath.

Simple Chow-Chow

A delicious recipe to serve with meats and beans!

2 large heads cabbage
1½ pounds green bell peppers, chopped
4 sweet red bell peppers, chopped
4 medium green tomatoes, chopped
4 medium onions, chopped
1½ pints vinegar
3 cups sugar

Chop cabbage and add 4 teaspoons salt. Working with your hands, mix and squeeze until a bit of juice comes from cabbage.

Add chopped peppers and tomatoes. Work a bit more and add chopped onions.

Mix vinegar, 1½ pints water, 4½ teaspoons salt and sugar. Pour over chopped vegetable ingredients. Bring to a rolling boil and cook for 5 minutes after boil begins.

Pour into hot sterilized jars* to within ½ inch of top, wipe rims clean and screw on lids.

Place jars in water bath** to cover and heat in boiling water for at least 10 minutes. Cool before tightening lids completely. Makes about 14 pints.

*Page 163: Instructions for sterilizing jars and lids.
**Page 163-165: Instructions for water bath.

Salsa, Sauces & Juice

Contents

Chunky Salsa

6 pounds tomatoes, blanched, peeled, minced*
2 green bell peppers, cored, seeded, minced
2 red bell peppers, cored, seeded, minced
3 white onions, minced
1 large bunch cilantro, snipped
2 (7 ounce) cans diced green chilies with liquid
2 - 3 tablespoons minced garlic
1 tablespoon ground cumin
3 cups (5% acidity) apple cider vinegar
¾ cup lime juice
1½ teaspoons pickling salt

● Combine all ingredients in large saucepan and bring
to a boil. Reduce heat and simmer for 10 minutes.
Pour into hot sterilized jars** to within ½ inch of top,
wipe rims clean and screw on lids.

● Place jars in water bath*** to cover and heat in
boiling water for at least 10 minutes. Cool before
tightening lids completely. Makes about 9 pints.

*TIP: Blanch tomatoes by dipping in boiling water for a
few seconds; then dip in cold water to slip skins off.

**Page 163: Instructions for sterilizing jars and lids.
***Page 163-165: Instructions for water bath.

Backyard Barbecue Sauce

1 cup tomato ketchup
¾ cup packed brown sugar
½ cup corn oil (not other vegetable oil)
¼ cup vinegar
3 tablespoons Worcestershire sauce
¼ cup chili powder
1 tablespoon prepared mustard

Combine all ingredients and stir well. Pour into hot sterilized pint jar* to within ½ inch of top, wipe rim clean and screw on lid.

Place jar in water bath** to cover and heat in boiling water for at least 10 minutes. Cool before tightening lid completely. Makes about 1 pint.

*Page 163: Instructions for sterilizing jars and lids.
**Page 163-165: Instructions for water bath.

*Underripe fruit will make jelly too thick
and overripe fruit will make jelly too runny.*

Grandma's Secret Barbecue Sauce

1 cup white vinegar
½ cup sugar
3 (32 ounce) cans tomato sauce
3 (28 ounce) cans whole tomatoes, pureed
1 tablespoon pickling salt
3 large onions, minced
1 pound jalapenos, seeded, chopped
5 - 7 cloves garlic, minced

Combine vinegar, sugar, tomato sauce and pureed tomatoes in saucepan with 1 cup water and pickling salt; bring to a boil. Add remaining ingredients.

Cook on medium for 30 to 45 minutes; stir continuously to prevent scorching or sticking. Pour into hot sterilized jars* to within ½ inch of top, wipe rims clean and screw on lids.

Place jars in water bath** to cover and heat in boiling water for at least 10 minutes. Cool before tightening lids completely. Makes about 10 to 12 pints.

*Page 163: Instructions for sterilizing jars and lids.
**Page 163-165: Instructions for water bath.

Old-Fashioned Chili Sauce

6½ pounds ripe tomatoes, diced
½ - 1 large white onion, minced
1½ cups sugar
1 teaspoon nutmeg
¾ teaspoon hot pepper sauce
½ teaspoon curry powder
2 cups vinegar
2 teaspoons ginger
1 teaspoon cinnamon
1 teaspoon dry mustard
5 teaspoons pickling salt

Prepare enough pureed tomatoes to equal 4 quarts and enough minced onion to equal ⅔ cup. Add all ingredients to large saucepan and gently boil for 2 hours; stir frequently to prevent scorching.

Pour into hot sterilized jars* to within ½ inch of top, wipe rims clean and screw on lids.

Place jars in water bath** to cover and heat in boiling water for at least 30 minutes. Cool before tightening lids completely. Makes about 4 to 6 quarts or 8 to 12 pints.

*Page 163: Instructions for sterilizing jars and lids.
**Page 163-165: Instructions for water bath.

Hot Chihuahua Picante Sauce

About 24 ripe tomatoes, peeled, cored, chopped
2 - 2½ large white onions, minced
6 - 8 medium jalapenos, seeded, minced
1 cup sugar
2½ cups vinegar
3 tablespoons pickling salt

Prepare enough chopped tomatoes to equal 4 quarts, enough minced onions to equal 2 cups and enough minced jalapenos to equal 1 to 1½ cups.

Combine all ingredients in large saucepan, cook on low for about 45 minutes; stir frequently. Pour into hot sterilized jars* to within ½ inch of top, wipe rims clean and screw on lids.

Place jars in water bath** to cover and heat in boiling water for at least 10 minutes. Cool before tightening lids completely. Makes about 6 pints.

*Page 163: Instructions for sterilizing jars and lids.
**Page 163-165: Instructions for water bath.

Homemade Ketchup

10 - 15 pounds tomatoes, peeled, pureed
2 cups sugar
1 cup white vinegar
1 tablespoon ground cinnamon
1 tablespoon dry mustard
Red food coloring, optional

Puree enough tomatoes to equal 5 quarts. Combine tomatoes, sugar and vinegar in large saucepan. Make seasoning bag out of thin cloth, add spices and close securely.

Add to saucepan and cook over medium low heat until mixture reaches desired consistency. Stir frequently so mixture will not stick to bottom of pan.

Remove seasoning bag and add red food coloring if needed. Pour into hot sterilized jars* to within ½ inch of top, wipe rims clean and screw on lids.

Place jars in water bath** to cover and heat in boiling water for at least 10 minutes. Cool before tightening lids completely. Makes about 4 quarts.

*Page 163: Instructions for sterilizing jars and lids.
**Page 163-165: Instructions for water bath.

Homemade Vegetable Juice

2 - 3 pounds tomatoes, peeled, pureed
4 ribs celery, pureed
2 bell peppers, cored, seeded, pureed
1 large onion, pureed
1 jalapeno, seeded, pureed, optional

🍅 Puree enough tomatoes to equal 2 quarts tomato juice. Pour into large saucepan with remaining ingredients and bring to a boil. Remove from heat and pour through strainer.

🍅 Cook again until it boils. Pour into hot sterilized jars* to within ½ inch of top, wipe rims clean and screw on lids.

🍅 Place jars in water bath** to cover and heat in boiling water for at least 20 minutes. Cool before tightening lids completely. Makes about 2 to 3 quarts or 4 to 6 pints.

*Page 163: Instructions for sterilizing jars and lids.
**Page 163-165: Instructions for water bath.

What do you call cattle with a sense of humor?

Laughingstock.

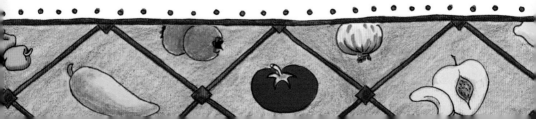

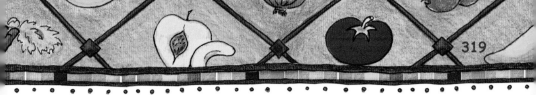

End of Garden Canning

End of Garden Canning

*When the garden is down to its last hurrah,
just put what's left in a jar. You don't lose
any produce and you get beautiful jars
filled with interesting shapes, sizes and
colors of your favorite fruits and vegetables.*

Fruits and vegetables
2½ cups vinegar
2 - 3 cloves garlic
¼ cup pickling salt

Place fruits and vegetables into hot sterilized
pint jars*.

Add vinegar, garlic and pickling salt to 2½ cups water
in saucepan and bring to a rolling boil.

Pour over fruits and vegetables in hot sterilized jars*
to within ½ inch of top. Wipe rims clean and screw
on lids.

Place jars in water bath** to cover and heat in boiling
water for 35 minutes for pint jars and 45 minutes for
quart jars. Cool before tightening lids completely.
Makes 2 pints.

*Page 163: Instructions for sterilizing jars and lids.
**Page 163-165: Instructions for water bath.

Bibliography

A Texas Hill Country Cookbook
Blue-Lake-Deerhaven Cookbook
Committee Marble Falls, Texas 1976

Ball Blue Book: Guide to Preserving.
Altrista Consumer Products. 2004.

Ball Complete Book of Home Preserving.
Judi Kingry and Lauren Devine.
Robert Rose, Publisher. 2006.

Big Basic Cookbook. Revised by
Kimberley Beeman. Mud Puddle
Books. New York, New York. 2007.

*Complete Guide to Home Canning
and Preserving.* U.S. Department
of Agriculture. Revised 2009.
bnpublishing.net.

Consumer's Dictionary of Food Additives.
Ruth Winter, M.S. Three Rivers
Press. New York, New York. 1994.

Easy Cooking with 5 Ingredients.
Barbara C. Jones. Cookbook
Resources, LLC. Highland Village,
Texas. 2002.

Food Lover's Companion. Sharon Tyler
Herbst. Barron's Educational Series,
Inc. 2001.

Frances Parkinson Keyes Cookbook.
Frances Parkinson Keyes. Doubleday
and Company. Garden City, New
York. 1955.

Great Health Hints and Handy Tips.
Reader's Digest. The Reader's Digest
Association, Inc. Pleasantville, New
York/Montreal. 1994.

I'll Have What They Are Having. Linda
Stradley. Three Forks, Globe Pequot
Press. Guilford, Connecticut. 2002.

Leaving Home. Louise P. Grace, R.D.
Bonham, Texas. 1984.

Let's Eat at Home. Julie Bennell.
Thomas Y. Crowell Company. New
York, New York. 1961.

*Pickles and Relishes: From Apples to
Zucchinis*, Andrea Chesman. Storey
Publishing. 1991.

Rogue River Rendezvous. Junior League
of Medford, Oregon. The Wimmer
Companies.

*The 1896 Boston Cooking-School Cook
Book.* Fannie Merritt Farmer.
Gramercy Books. New York, New
York. 1997.

The American Table. Ronald Johnson.
Silver Spring Books. Weston,
Connecticut. 2000.

*The Complete Book of Small Batch
Preserving.* Ellie Topp and Margaret
Howard. Firefly Books. 2007.

The Oxford Companion to Food. Alan
Davidson. Oxford University Press.
New York, New York. 2007.

The Rituals of Dinner. Margaret Visser.
Penguin Books. New York, New
York. 1991.

The Ultimate Cooking with 4 Ingredients.
Jean Coates. Cookbook Resources,
LLC. Highland Village, Texas. 2002

The Vegetable Gardener's Bible. Edward
C. Smith. Storey Books. Pownal,
Vermont. 2000.

The Vitamin Book. Harold M.
Silverman. Bantam Books. New
York, New York. 1999.

You Can Can. A Visual Step-by-Step
Guide to Canning, Preserving and
Pickling. Better Homes and Gardens.
2010.

Additional References:

Ball Corporation.   http://
freshpreserving.com; www.ball.com

Burpee Seed Company.   www.burpee.
com

Enchanted Learning
www.enchantedlearning.com/usa/
states/

50 States.com   50states.com

National Center for Home Food
Preservation   http://nchfp.uga.edu/

PickYourOwn.org   www.pickyourown.org

United States Department of
Agriculture.   http://usda.gov

Index

A

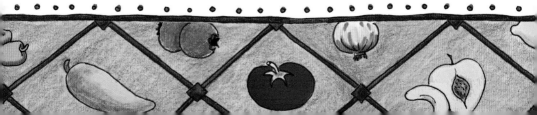

D

G

Cookbooks Published by Cookbook Resources, LLC
Bringing Family and Friends to the Table

The Best 1001 Short, Easy Recipes
1001 Slow Cooker Recipes
1001 Short, Easy, Inexpensive Recipes
1001 Fast Easy Recipes
1001 America's Favorite Recipes
1001 Easy Inexpensive Grilling Recipes
1,001 Easy Potluck Recipes
Easy Slow Cooker Cookbook
Busy Woman's Slow Cooker Recipes
Busy Woman's Quick & Easy Recipes
365 Easy Soups and Stews
365 Easy Chicken Recipes
365 Easy One-Dish Recipes
365 Easy Soup Recipes
365 Easy Vegetarian Recipes
365 Easy Casserole Recipes
365 Easy Pasta Recipes
365 Easy Slow Cooker Recipes
Super Simple Cupcake Recipes
Easy Garden Fresh Recipes & Homemade Preserves (Photos)
Easy Soups and Slow Cooker Recipes (Photos)
Leaving Home Cookbook and Survival Guide
Essential 3-4-5 Ingredient Recipes
Ultimate 4 Ingredient Cookbook
Easy Cooking with 5 Ingredients
The Best of Cooking with 3 Ingredients
Easy Diabetic Recipes
Ultimate 4 Ingredient Diabetic Cookbook
4-Ingredient Recipes for 30-Minute Meals
Cooking with Beer
The Washington Cookbook
The Pennsylvania Cookbook
The California Cookbook
Best-Loved Canadian Recipes
Best-Loved Recipes from the Pacific Northwest
Easy Homemade Preserves (Handbook with Photos)
Garden Fresh Recipes (Handbook with Photos)

Easy Garden Fresh Recipes & Homemade Preserves   335

Easy Garden Fresh Recipes & Homemade Preserves   335

Easy Slow Cooker Recipes (Handbook with Photos)
Cool Smoothies (Handbook with Photos)
Easy Cupcake Recipes (Handbook with Photos)
Easy Soup Recipes (Handbook with Photos)
Classic Tex-Mex and Texas Cooking
Best-Loved Southern Recipes
Classic Southwest Cooking
Miss Sadie's Southern Cooking
Classic Pennsylvania Dutch Cooking
The Quilters' Cookbook
Healthy Cooking with 4 Ingredients
Trophy Hunter's Wild Game Cookbook
Recipe Keeper
Simple Old-Fashioned Baking
Quick Fixes with Cake Mixes
Kitchen Keepsakes & More Kitchen Keepsakes
Cookbook 25 Years
Texas Longhorn Cookbook
The Authorized Texas Ranger Cookbook
Gifts for the Cookie Jar
All New Gifts for the Cookie Jar
The Big Bake Sale Cookbook
Easy One-Dish Meals
Easy Potluck Recipes
Easy Casseroles Cookbook
Easy Desserts
Sunday Night Suppers
Easy Church Suppers
365 Easy Meals
Gourmet Cooking with 5 Ingredients
Muffins In A Jar
A Little Taste of Texas
A Little Taste of Texas II
Ultimate Gifts for the Cookie Jar

**cookbook
resources** LLC

www.cookbookresources.com
Toll-Free 866-229-2665
Your Ultimate Source for Easy Cookbooks

Easy Soup and Slow Cooker Recipes is filled with delicious, easy, comforting foods that save you time and bring smiles to the faces around your kitchen table. These home-cooked favorites are easy to prepare and fun for family and friends to come home to.

- Easy prep... Everyday ingredients
  - Great for quick meals and even better leftovers
    - Fun to home come to delicious slow cooker recipes

Easy Garden Fresh Recipes & Homemade Preserves is the best cookbook to find easy, delicious recipes with fresh ingredients from your garden or farmers' markets. The easy canning recipes help you preserve those fresh ingredients for year-round pleasure from the season's best buys.

- Easy, delicious recipes serve up the best homemade memories.
  - Great flavors of fresh foods that are safe from preservatives. Know where your food comes from.
    - Simple water bath canning makes the pressure cooker old-fashioned.
      - Fresh Is Best!

Memories are made in the kitchen.

See our full catalog and Web site at www.cookbookresources.com or call toll-free at 866-229-2665.

Bringing Family and Friends to the Table